500

fish & shellfish dishes

500

fish & shellfish dishes

the only compendium of fish & shellfish dishes you'll ever need

Judith M. Fertig

SELLERS

PUBLISHING

A Quintet Book

Published by Sellers Publishing, Inc.
161 John Roberts Road, South Portland, Maine 04106
For ordering information:
(800) 625-3386 Toll Free
(207) 772-6814 Fax
Visit our Web site: www.sellerspublishing.com
E-mail: rsp@rsvp.com

ISBN: 978-1-4162-0621-7
Library of Congress Control Number: 2010932866
QTT.FSD

This book was conceived, designed, and produced by
Quintet Publishing Limited
6 Blundell Street
London N7 9BH
United Kingdom

Food Stylist: Valentina Sforza
Photographer: Ian Garlick
Designer: Mat Deaves
Art Director: Michael Charles
Editorial Assistant: Holly Willsher
Managing Editor: Donna Gregory
Publisher: James Tavendale

10 9 8 7 6 5 4 3 2 1

Printed in China by 1010 Printing International Ltd.

contents

introduction   6

raw bar   22

all steamed up   48

simmered   74

into the frying pan   100

in the oven   126

on the grill   152

on a plank   178

roasted   204

in the smoker   230

sauces & sides   256

index & credits   282

introduction

If there is one food that most people hesitate to add to their culinary repertoire, it's probably seafood. But it's really a very simple food to prepare, and you'll get heartfelt compliments every time you do it.

This book helps demystify preparing and cooking seafood. Whether you wish to eat your seafood as is—oysters on the half shell, gravlax, sushi, or crudo, for example—or you prefer to cook it in any number of ways, *500 Fish & Shellfish Dishes* has a recipe and a technique for you.

Long ago, the only fish or shellfish available to cooks was the locally caught variety or preserved seafood, such as salted and dried cod in European cuisine, smoked fish in Africa, or dried shrimp in Chinese culture. The problem was transportation. Fish and shellfish are very perishable and can go from delicate and briny to mushy with the "off" aroma of ammonia in a day or so.

Today, seafood is shipped, iced-down, from coast to coast on the same day it's caught. You can also buy "FAS," fish and shellfish that have been "frozen at sea," the same day they're caught. Freshwater catfish or farmed shrimp can be "IQF" or "individually quick frozen." Catfish farmers in the Mississippi Delta can net a catfish pond and transport the fish in a tank truck to the processing plant nearby, where the fish go from whole fish to frozen fillets in a matter of hours.

what is fresh?

So, what is fresh? Freshness is apparent in the smell, texture, and taste, not always in the state in which seafood is offered for sale.

In a blind taste test from the Chef's Collaborative, a group of culinary professionals sampled simply prepared fish and shellfish—some of it "fresh" and never frozen, some of it frozen at sea. Sometimes, the frozen-at-sea product was better. If you recall the film *The Perfect Storm*, you remember that they had been fishing for days and had iced down the swordfish. If they had returned to port safely, the swordfish would have been several days old already. Is that fresh?

To further complicate matters, fish that is offered for sale "fresh" at many grocery stores has actually been thawed from frozen.

Whether the seafood you're buying is fresh or thawed from frozen, the best way to determine freshness is with your eyes and nose, so go to a quality fish market—don't buy fish at a supermarket unless you are absolutely certain they have top-quality fish. Don't be afraid to ask the fishmonger if you can smell or touch the fish before you buy.

* Whole fish should have clear eyes and a briny, fresh aroma.
* Clams, mussels, and oysters should have tightly closed shells and a briny aroma.
* Fish fillets and steaks should be delicate yet firm and have a sweet, briny aroma.

* Squid, calamari, and octopus should be firm to the touch and have a sweet, briny aroma.
* Sea or bay scallops out of the shell as well as shrimp should be firm to the touch and have a sweet, briny aroma.
* Crabs, crayfish, langoustines, and lobsters should be alive and moving, or cooked, with their meat picked out of the shell and chilled, canned, or frozen.

seafood substitution chart

Use this guide to help you select the freshest fish and shellfish at the market. If your seafood choice is not available, substitute another fish/shellfish from the same category. Also, if a fish is endangered, substitute one that is abundant.

	mild flavor	moderate flavor	full flavor
firm texture	lobster	john dory	cuttlefish
	monkfish	salmon	escolar
	sea bass	shark	ono
	shrimp	skate	marlin
	softshell crab	sturgeon	squid
	prawns	swordfish	tuna
	halibut	cobia	oysters
medium-firm texture	catfish	arctic char	amberjack
	grouper	barracuda	mullet
	haddock	mahi mahi	kingfish
	halibut	porgy	mackerel
	ocean perch	trout	permit
	pompano	salmon fillet	sablefish
	scallops	tilapia	yellowtail jack
	snapper	walleye pike	yellowtail snapper
	striped bass		wahoo
	tilefish		
	whitefish		
	wolffish		
delicate texture	bass (freshwater)	butterfish	anchovies
	cod	herring	bluefish
	flounder	pomfret	buffalofish
	fluke	shad	sardines
	hake	smelt/whitebait	
	pink snapper		
	red snapper		
	sand dab		
	turbot		

equipment

Seafood can be prepared with the usual indoor kitchen equipment: blender or food processor, chopping board and knives, measuring cups and spoons, pots and pans, garlic press, grater, wooden spoons, etc. Outdoors, a simple barbecue grill with a lid and barbecue equipment such as grill tongs and spatula are enough to get you started. But if you want to take a very authentic approach to global seafood cuisine, you might want to check out the following kitchen helpers.

deep-fryer
With a deep-fryer, you can set the temperature, heat the oil, and fry seafood in an exact yet effortless way.

grill wok
This metal wok, with perforations to let the grill flavors reach the food, allows you to stir-grill seafood, turning the food with wooden paddles or long-handled, metal grill spatulas.

hardwood chips
Bags of hardwood chips—apple, mesquite, hickory, etc.—are available at hardware, grocery, or big box stores in the barbecue section. Use a handful to create a "kiss of smoke" for your seafood.

hardwood planks

Thin grilling or thick oven planks made from cedar, alder, maple, or oak are used to plank-cook seafood on the grill or in the oven.

oyster knife

With heavy gloves and a sturdy, wide-bladed oyster knife, you can learn to open the most uncooperative oyster.

stovetop smoker

This metal pan with a lid and a handle allows you to smoke foods indoors on your stovetop. You place a small amount of very fine wood chips in the center of the bottom, cover with the tray, place the food on a rack on the tray, then close the lid to smoke. Small foods like fish fillets or shrimp can be smoked in minutes this way.

sushi mat

The sushi mat is a simple woven bamboo rectangle. You layer your sushi ingredients on the mat, then use its sturdiness to help you roll the delicate ingredients together.

thermometer

A candy thermometer, clipped to the side of a pan of oil, will let you know the temperature of the oil so seafood fries up crisp and golden.

seafood preparation tips

There are a variety of ways to prepare seafood, but there are a few basic guidelines to follow, whatever method you use:

* For food safety reasons, keep fish and shellfish—especially shellfish—chilled until you're ready to serve raw or cook.

* When in doubt, go for underdone. Fish and shellfish continue to cook for a minute or so more, away from the heat, and that can make a big difference, so pull them off the heat a minute or so before you're sure they're done. Worse case scenario? The seafood is a bit undercooked, and you can put it back in the poacher, in the oven, or on the grill to get it more done if necessary. But once it's overcooked, there's nothing you can do.

* Understand which is the skin side and the flesh side on fish fillets. Even when the skin has been removed from a fish fillet, you can still see darkened areas where it used to be. So when you follow the directions for grilling or planking fish, you'll know which side is which.

frying

Fish fillets and shellfish take best to frying. Fish steaks tend to curl up and whole fish do best deep-fried, but they require a big pan and a lot of oil. Thinner fillets like sole can be sautéed, while thicker fillets such as cod taste great with a batter and deep-fried.

Rinse and pat dry the seafood before adding any batter or coating. Make sure the oil is hot—about 375°F—before you start frying. Do a test run with a small piece of bread if you're not sure. If the bread starts to sizzle and bubble around the edges as soon as it hits the oil, you're ready. You can also invest in a candy thermometer or use a temperature-controlled deep fryer to gauge the temperature of the oil. Seafood is done when it is golden brown on all sides. Larger pieces of fish or shellfish will need to be turned as soon as one side is golden brown. When the seafood is done, remove it with a slotted spoon or pancake turner to drain on paper towels.

Grilling fish fillets—the more delicate flesh-side down first, then flipping over to the sturdier skin-side—helps the fillets stay together better. Only turn them once, using a wide-bladed fish spatula.

The hot fire is actually better for grilling fish, as the surface gets crusty fast and makes fillets easier to turn with the help of a fish spatula—one with a wider metal spatula end.

grilling

A hot fire, some oil or melted butter, and the seasoning or marinade of your choice are all you need to grill perfect fish and shellfish. The hot fire makes the surface get crusty quickly (with fillets, start with the delicate flesh-side down first, which helps the fillet stay together), and then you flip the fish over—just once—with a wide-bladed fish spatula. The fat, such as olive oil or melted butter, helps keep seafood from drying out during grilling and keeps it from sticking to the grill. The marinade imbues seafood with flavor—but just be careful not to marinate fish or shellfish for more than 30 minutes in an acidic marinade or you could end up with ceviche—delicious, but not what you were intending when you fired up the grill.

Grill most fish fillets over a hot fire for 10 minutes per inch of thickness—measure the thickness in the thickest part of the fillet before you grill. Fillets are generally 3/4 inch thick, so the total grilling time would be 7 1/2 minutes or about 3–4 minutes per side. The exception is meaty fish such as tuna, swordfish, and shark, which many people like to eat rare to medium. These types of fish will be well-done over a hot fire in 6–7 minutes per inch of thickness. They tend to overcook and dry out more quickly than other fish. If you want a rare tuna steak, grill it for 1–2 minutes per side over a hot fire.

If you think your fish is very delicate, use a perforated grill rack, and oil both the fish and the grill rack before you cook.

If you're a novice and worried about your skills, start out with inexpensive, medium-textured, farm-raised catfish for practice.

oven-baking & roasting

You can bake almost any type of fish and shellfish, from fish fillets and steaks to whole fish, to shellfish of all kinds. Generally, baking is done at a temperature around 350°F until the seafood is lightly browned and done. A relatively short baking time and buttery moisture keeps fish and shellfish tender and succulent in the oven.

Roasting, usually done at temperatures above 400°F, works best with shrimp, oysters, whole fish, and thicker fish fillets. Fish steaks tend to curl up when roasted, and thin fish fillets are better broiled, planked, baked, or sautéed. As you would for grilling, brush seafood with a fat such as olive oil or butter or a sauce to help keep it from drying out for the brief time it's in the oven.

planking

Planking is the simplest way to cook on the grill—just place the seafood on a plank on the grill and close the lid. With planked seafood, you get the gentle, aromatic flavor of the wood quite different from the flavor of grilling or smoking. You prepare an indirect fire, with the heat on one side and no heat on the other. The plank goes on the side with no heat. Basically, there are two types of hardwood planks that work well on the grill. Flat, thin planks (usually sold in packages) are for cooking foods without drizzly sauces that might drip and cause flare-ups on the grill. Thicker cedar oven planks with a well in the center can also be used on the grill and work well for seafood dishes with lots of butter or sauces. Make sure you soak the plank (thick or thin) in cold water for at least 30 minutes before putting it on the grill.

poaching, steaming & simmering

Water that is gently simmering is kinder to delicate fish and shellfish and results in better texture than boiling water, which makes seafood more rubbery. When making a seafood soup or stew, you generally start by building flavor in the broth, adding and cooking vegetables under tender, then adding the fish and shellfish toward the end of cooking so that they don't cook any longer than necessary.

serving fish raw

Raw fish should be as fresh as possible. "Sashimi grade" is the highest-quality raw fish you can buy, so go for that grade when you want to serve it. To cut fish into really thin slices for crudo or sushi, freeze a whole piece of fish for 30 minutes or so, then slice with a sharp knife. Keep all raw fish or shellfish chilled until ready to serve.

smoking

There are two ways to smoke fish and shellfish. Cold smoking preserves seafood, but doesn't cook it; cold smoking requires special equipment. Hot smoking cooks seafood, but doesn't preserve it; you can hot smoke on your grill or in a stovetop smoker. The recipes in this book are for hot smoking. To hot smoke seafood, you need to prepare an indirect fire in your grill. This means the fire is on one side of the grill only. Then add wood to the fire so that it smolders and smokes. For a charcoal grill, add hardwood chips to the hot coals. For a gas grill, place them in a metal smoker box or an aluminum foil packet with holes poked in it, and set it close to a flame. To cook, place your seafood on the no-heat side of the grill. When you see the first wisp of smoke, close the grill to smoke your food.

raw bar

Every culture has its own delicious way to enjoy
uncooked seafood—gravlax in Scandinavia, sushi in
Japan, ceviche in Peru, crudo in Italy. Served on a
chilled plate or in a cocktail glass, raw fish looks and
tastes wonderful garnished with herbs, spices, or a
drizzle of sauce.

oysters on the half shell

see variations page 38

From Belon (France) to Blue Point (New England), Sydney Rock (Australia and New Zealand), or Kumamoto (California), oyster varieties differ in size, brininess, and flavor depending on their oceanic region. Have your fishmonger open the oysters for you or wear heavy gloves and use an oyster knife to pry the mollusks apart—right before serving. Dip each oyster into your favorite sauce or simply enjoy with a squeeze of fresh lemon.

for the mignonette sauce
1 cup dry white wine
1/2 cup red wine vinegar
1/4 cup minced shallots
1 1/2 tsp. black peppercorns, crushed
1/8 tsp. salt

rock salt
2 dozen fresh oysters on the half shell
fresh lemon wedges, to garnish

Whisk the wine and wine vinegar together in a small saucepan and bring to a boil. Cook until reduced to 3/4 cup (about 5 minutes). Stir in shallots, peppercorns, and salt. Chill 2 hours.

Cover a platter with rock salt, 1 inch deep. Arrange the chilled oysters on the rock salt and garnish with lemon wedges. Portion sauce into 4 dipping sauce bowls. Serve immediately.

Serves 4

fresh tuna carpaccio

see variations page 39

Thin slices of raw tuna, drizzled with a zesty sauce, make for a colorful and pleasing appetizer platter. Based on a raw beef dish named after the fifteenth-century artist Vittore Carpaccio and served at Harry's Bar in Venice, tuna carpaccio looks as good as it tastes. Sashimi-grade indicates the freshest, best-quality fish meant to be eaten raw.

1/2–1 lb. sashimi-grade tuna, cut 1 inch thick,
    skin removed, rinsed, and patted dry
3/4 cup good-quality mayonnaise
1 tbsp. grainy mustard

2 tbsp. fresh lemon juice
extra-virgin olive oil
1 tbsp. capers, drained, to garnish
coarse kosher or sea salt to taste

Wrap and chill the tuna in the freezer for an hour or two, until it is stiff but not frozen through. Slice it horizontally into four 1/4-inch-thick pieces. Put a slice of tuna between two pieces of waxed paper and pound gently from the center outward, until about 1/8 inch thick. Repeat with the other slices. Place the slices, still in the waxed paper, in the refrigerator until ready to serve.

Whisk the mayonnaise, mustard, and lemon juice together in a bowl until smooth. Spoon into a sealable plastic bag. To serve, drizzle the olive oil on a platter and top with the tuna pieces. Snip a bottom corner of the plastic bag and squeeze a pattern of carpaccio sauce over the tuna. Garnish with capers and a sprinkle of salt.

Serves 4

asian raw fish salad

see variations page 40

Known in China as yu sheng or yee sheng, and translated as "rainbow raw fish salad," this dish has a wonderful variety of colors, tastes, and textures. Use the method for cutting thin slices of tuna carpaccio, then vary the other ingredients by season or preference.

for the marinade
8 oz. tuna or yellowtail, thinly
    sliced (see method on page
    24), rinsed and patted dry
1 (1-inch) piece fresh
    gingerroot, shredded
1 tsp. soy sauce
1 tbsp. toasted sesame oil

for the vinaigrette
1 (1-inch) piece fresh
    gingerroot, shredded
1/4 cup unseasoned rice wine
    vinegar
juice of 1 lime
2 tbsp. vegetable oil
2 tsp. soy sauce
1 tbsp. toasted sesame seeds

for the salad
1 cup shredded carrots
1 cup thinly sliced cucumber
2 heads baby bok choy,
    separated into leaves
2 red bell peppers, seeded and
    thinly sliced
fresh cilantro, to garnish

Tear the tuna slices into small pieces and arrange in a flat dish. Whisk the gingerroot, soy sauce, and sesame oil together and pour over the fish. Let marinate while you make the vinaigrette. For the vinaigrette, whisk the gingerroot, rice vinegar, lime juice, oil, soy sauce, and sesame seeds together in a bowl; set aside.

Arrange mounds of carrots, cucumber, bok choy, and bell peppers around the rim of a large platter. Mound the marinated tuna in the middle. Drizzle the vinaigrette over all and garnish with cilantro. Serve immediately.

Serves 6

sashimi

see variations page 41

Easier and simpler to make than sushi, sashimi is simply raw fish cut into thin, small pieces and served with a fresh vegetable relish. Sashimi-grade indicates the freshest, best-quality fish meant to be eaten raw.

8 oz. fresh amberjack, tuna, salmon, or trout
   fillet, skin removed, rinsed, and patted dry
1 cup freshly grated carrots
1 cup freshly grated daikon

mizuna leaves, to garnish
soy sauce, pickled gingerroot, and wasabi,
   to serve

Wrap and chill the fish in the freezer for an hour or two, until it is stiff but not frozen through. With a very sharp knife, cut the fillet on the diagonal into 1/4-inch-thick slices. Divide and arrange the slices on 4 plates. Arrange the grated carrots, daikon, and mizuna on each plate. Serve with soy sauce, pickled gingerroot, and wasabi.

Serves 4

halibut crudo

see variations page 42

Crudo is the Italian version of sashimi, usually made with thinly sliced raw fish, extra-virgin olive oil, a drizzle of lemon juice, and fresh herbs. Like sushi, crudo offers a wealth of choices, so feel free to create your own version. Just make sure the fish is very thinly sliced and attractive on the plate. Sashimi-grade indicates the freshest, best-quality fish meant to be eaten raw.

8 oz. sashimi-grade halibut fillet, skin removed, rinsed, and patted dry
extra-virgin olive oil for drizzling

coarse kosher or sea salt
1 lemon, cut into 8 wedges
fresh basil or mint leaves, to garnish

Wrap and chill the halibut in the freezer for an hour or two, until it is stiff but not frozen through. Slice it horizontally—across the grain—into eight 1/8-inch-thick pieces. Drizzle olive oil on each of 4 plates. Arrange the fish on the olive oil and sprinkle with salt. Place 2 lemon wedges on each plate and scatter fresh basil or mint leaves over all. Keep chilled before serving.

Serves 4

simple sushi

see variations page 43

To make simple sushi, you roll up bite-sized pieces of raw fish and seasoned sushi rice in roasted seaweed wrappers known as nori. You'll need a sushi mat—a small, flexible rectangle made from thin pieces of bamboo—to help you roll everything together. You make the sushi right before you're ready to serve it, as the seaweed wrappers can be tough to chew if they get soggy.

4 oz. fish fillets, such as tuna, mackerel, salmon, or halibut, rinsed and patted dry
1 (8 1/2–7 1/2-inch) nori

1 cup cooked sushi rice
soy sauce, pickled gingerroot, and prepared wasabi, to serve

Cut the fish into thin, finger-sized pieces. Lay a sheet of nori, shiny-side down, on the sushi mat. Gently spread the sushi rice over the wrapper, leaving a 1-inch border at the top. In the center of the rice, lay a horizontal band of raw fish. Starting at the top, use the sushi mat to help you roll the sushi so that it is firm but not tight, making sure the rice does not come out at the ends. Remove the sushi roll from the mat and cut it into 8 pieces. Serve the sushi with small bowls of soy sauce, pickled gingerroot, and wasabi for dipping.

Serves 4

gravlax

see variations page 44

With its silken texture and fresh flavor, thinly sliced gravlax makes a wonderful appetizer or first course with buttered brown or rye bread. Gravlax is a Scandinavian specialty of fresh salmon cured in a mixture of sugar, salt, and herbs for a succulent finish. Gravlax freezes well for up to 3 months.

3 lbs. salmon fillet, preferably the center cut,
   skin removed, rinsed, and patted dry
1/4 cup fine kosher salt

1/4 cup sugar
1 1/2 cups freshly chopped dill (tops and stems)
1 tsp. freshly ground black pepper

Remove any stray bones from the fillet with tweezers. Pat the fillet dry again. Combine the salt, sugar, dill, and pepper in a bowl. Rub the flesh side of the salmon with the mixture. Place salmon in a baking pan to catch the juices. Cover with plastic wrap. Place a brick or a heavy can on top of the salmon. Refrigerate for 72 hours.

When ready to serve, discard the liquid in the bottom of the pan. Scrape off most of the topping, slice the salmon very thinly on the diagonal, and serve. Gravlax keeps in the refrigerator, well wrapped, for up to 1 week. If you want to freeze it, separate the slices with pieces of waxed or parchment paper, then package and freeze.

Serves 8–10

peruvian ceviche

see variations page 45

The Pacific coast of Peru is famous for its marinated raw fish dish known as ceviche. Basically, small pieces of raw fish are "cooked" in citrus juice or vinegar enlivened with other flavorings, then served chilled in a small bowl or on ceviche spoons.

12 oz. fresh swordfish, tuna, or mahi mahi,
    rinsed, patted dry, and cut into small cubes
1/2 cup fresh lime juice
2 tbsp. fresh orange juice
1 tsp. ground cumin

salt and ground white pepper to taste
1 cup seeded and finely chopped watermelon
1/2 cup freshly grated jicama
1/2 cup finely chopped green onion
1/2 cup finely chopped and peeled ripe tomato

Put the fish in a large glass or ceramic bowl. Add the lime and orange juices, cumin, salt, and white pepper. Mix well and cover tightly with plastic wrap. Refrigerate for 15 minutes.

Unwrap, then stir in the watermelon, jicama, onion, and tomato. Cover tightly again and refrigerate for 15 more minutes or until the fish is turning opaque on the outside but is still rare on the inside. Serve chilled.

Serves 8

snapper aotearoa

see variations page 46

Aotearoa is the Maori name for New Zealand. Of the 1,000 varieties of New Zealand saltwater fish, the best known and most prized is snapper, a favorite of recreational anglers. You can also use yellowtail kingfish, red snapper, or John Dory fillets in this marinated raw fish recipe, which is perfect for replacing a shrimp cocktail or for serving over salad greens.

2 lbs. snapper fillets, skin removed, rinsed, patted dry, and cut into 1/2-inch cubes
juice of 2 lemons
juice of 1 lime
1 medium red onion, very thinly sliced
1 red or yellow bell pepper, seeded and very thinly sliced

1 green bell pepper, seeded and very thinly sliced
1 cup cherry tomatoes, stems removed and cut in half
1 (14.5-oz.) can coconut milk
fine kosher or sea salt to taste

Place the cubed fish in a glass or ceramic bowl. Squeeze the citrus juice over the fish. Cover with plastic wrap and let stand in the refrigerator until the fish whitens, about 4–8 hours. Stir in the vegetables and coconut milk. Add salt to taste. Serve in cocktail glasses or over greens.

Serves 6

yellowtail tartare in tortilla cones

see variations page 47

Simple fish recipes like this one allow you time to create a more interesting presentation. The small tortilla cones are easy to make. See the recipes on page 47 for even more colorful and interesting presentation ideas, like contemporary paintings on a plate.

4 (10-inch) flour tortillas
4 oz. yellowtail or tuna steak, skin removed,
    rinsed, patted dry, and finely chopped
2 plum tomatoes, seeded and finely chopped
1 green onion, finely chopped

1/4 cup fresh lime juice
1/4 cup finely chopped fresh cilantro
2 tsp. vegetable oil
1/4 tsp. bottled hot pepper sauce

Preheat the oven to 350°F. Using a 3-inch round cookie cutter, cut 5 circles from each tortilla. Form each circle into a cone, securing the base with a toothpick. Place on a cookie sheet and bake for 10 minutes or until lightly browned and crisp. Let cool.

For the tartare, combine the remaining ingredients in a glass or ceramic bowl and gently stir to blend. Cover and chill for 1 to 24 hours. To serve, drain excess juice from the tartare. Spoon the tartare into each cone and serve on a platter.

Serves 4

oysters on the half shell

see base recipe page 23

sea scallops on the half shell
Prepare basic recipe, using sea scallops in place of oysters.

oysters with pickled gingerroot, wasabi & miso-soy sauce
Replace mignonette sauce with miso-soy dipping sauce. In saucepan, whisk 1/4 cup packed brown sugar, 2 tablespoons soy sauce, 2 tablespoons hot water, and 2 tablespoons miso. Boil, then chill for 2 hours. Prepare oysters, and add 1 tablespoon pickled gingerroot and 1 teaspoon prepared wasabi to each plate.

oysters with horseradish sauce
Replace mignonette sauce with horseradish sauce. Whisk 1 cup ketchup, 2 tablespoons prepared horseradish, 1/2 teaspoon bottled hot pepper sauce, 1/2 teaspoon Worcestershire sauce, and 1 tablespoon fresh lime juice.

grilled oysters with salsa verde
Instead of basic recipe, whisk 1 cup canned tomatillos, 1/4 cup finely chopped green onion, 1 finely chopped jalapeño (seeded), 2 teaspoons fresh lime juice, and salt to taste. Prepare a hot fire. Drizzle each oyster on half shell with salsa verde, place on grill rack, cover, and grill 3–4 minutes or until oyster edges begin to curl. Garnish with limes.

fresh tuna carpaccio

see base recipe page 24

fresh salmon carpaccio
Prepare the basic recipe, using fresh salmon in place of tuna.

fresh tuna carpaccio with ginger–lime sauce
Prepare the basic recipe, but replace the carpaccio sauce with ginger-lime sauce. Whisk 3/4 cup mayonnaise with 2 tablespoons fresh lime juice, 2 tablespoons grated fresh gingerroot, and 1/4 teaspoon bottled hot sauce. Omit the capers.

fresh salmon carpaccio with aïoli
Prepare the basic recipe, using salmon in place of tuna and Aïoli (page 262) in place of carpaccio sauce. Use finely chopped, pitted Kalamata olives in place of capers.

fresh japanese-style tuna carpaccio
Prepare the basic recipe, but instead of the carpaccio sauce, whisk together 1/4 cup tahini, 1/4 cup unseasoned rice wine vinegar, 1/4 cup wasabi powder, 1 1/2 teaspoons Dijon mustard, 1 1/2 teaspoons brown sugar, and 1 tablespoon soy sauce. Omit capers.

variations

asian raw fish salad

see base recipe page 27

asian raw fish salad with pickled gingerroot
Prepare the basic recipe, adding 1 cup pickled gingerroot to the platter of salad ingredients.

asian raw salmon salad
Prepare the basic recipe, using salmon cut in the carpaccio style (page 24) in place of tuna.

asian smoked salmon salad
Prepare the basic recipe, using thin slices of smoked salmon in place of raw tuna.

asian raw fish salad with plum vinaigrette & wonton crisps
Prepare the basic recipe, adding 2 teaspoons Chinese plum sauce to the vinaigrette. Add 1 cup wonton crisps or chow mein noodles and 1 cup pickled gingerroot to the salad ingredients.

variations

sashimi

see base recipe page 28

seared sashimi
Instead of basic recipe, brush top of chilled fillet with 1 tablespoon canola oil. Heat a cast-iron skillet until very hot, add fish, oiled-side down, and sear for 1 minute. Slice thinly on diagonal and serve with lemon.

sashimi with hot sesame oil
Prepare basic recipe, omitting garnish. Arrange fish slices on 4 plates. Drizzle fish with juice of 1 orange and sprinkle with matchstick slices of fresh gingerroot. Heat 2 tablespoons canola oil and 1 teaspoon toasted sesame oil and drizzle over the fish. Top with chopped cilantro.

sashimi with garlic-soy sauce
Prepare basic recipe. Bring to a boil 3 tablespoons soy sauce, 1 tablespoon unseasoned rice wine vinegar, 1 1/2 teaspoons sugar, 1/2 teaspoon grated fresh gingerroot, 4 small minced cloves garlic, 1 teaspoon vegetable oil, and 1/2 teaspoon bottled hot sauce. Cool and serve as a dipping sauce.

squid sashimi
Instead of fillet, use 4 medium sashimi-grade squid, filleted and skinned. Wrap and freeze for 30 minutes until firm, slice thinly on the diagonal, and proceed with basic recipe.

halibut crudo

see base recipe page 30

bay scallop crudo
Prepare the basic recipe, using small bay scallops in place of halibut (no need to cut into smaller pieces) and fresh chervil or tarragon in place of the basil.

halibut crudo with pesto
Prepare the basic recipe, drizzling the raw fish with prepared pesto. Garnish with lemon wedges and fresh basil leaves.

swordfish crudo with tapenade
Prepare the basic recipe, using swordfish in place of halibut. Drizzle the raw fish with prepared tapenade. Garnish with lemon wedges and finely chopped, pitted Kalamata olives.

halibut crudo with lemon & black pepper
Prepare the basic recipe, adding a grating of fresh lemon zest and a sprinkling of black pepper on top of each serving.

salmon crudo with carpaccio sauce
Prepare the basic recipe, using salmon in place of halibut and flat-leaf parsley leaves instead of basil. Drizzle the raw fish with carpaccio sauce (page 24).

simple sushi

see base recipe page 31

easy california roll
Instead of basic recipe, lay a sheet of plastic wrap over the sushi mat and spread 1 cup sushi rice into a 7-inch square. Lay a sheet of nori, shiny-side up, on top of the rice, leaving a 1-inch border on top. Across the middle, lay a band of finger-sized pieces of avocado. Lay a band of cooked crabmeat on the avocado. Using sushi mat and plastic wrap, start rolling sushi into a log, removing the plastic wrap as you go. Cut into 8 pieces and serve.

cucumber sushi
Prepare basic recipe, adding finger-sized pieces of English cucumber next to the raw fish.

asparagus & shrimp sushi
Prepare basic recipe, using large cooked shrimp in place of raw fish and adding finger-sized pieces of steamed asparagus.

finger or "nigiri" sushi
Prepare basic recipe, omitting nori. Place 1/4 cup sushi rice in one hand. Add a small piece of raw fish. Dab fish with the wasabi. With your hands, cover fish with rice and form a cylinder shape. Repeat with the remaining fish and rice.

variations

gravlax

see base recipe page 32

dill & beet-cured gravlax
Prepare the basic recipe, adding 1 cup shredded beets and 1 teaspoon ground coriander to the topping ingredients.

seared gravlax
Prepare the basic recipe. After removing the gravlax from the refrigerator and brushing off most but not all of the topping, brush the top with 1 tablespoon canola oil. Heat a cast-iron skillet until very hot. Place the gravlax, topping-side down, in the hot skillet and sear for 1 minute. Slice on the diagonal and serve with lemon wedges.

gravlax with juniper berries
Prepare the basic recipe, adding 1/4 cup crushed juniper berries to the topping.

orange-zested gravlax
Prepare the basic recipe, adding 2 teaspoons grated fresh orange zest and 1 teaspoon grated fresh lemon zest to the topping.

peruvian ceviche

see base recipe page 34

fresh tilapia ceviche
Prepare the basic recipe, using fresh tilapia.

fresh tuna ceviche
Prepare the basic recipe, using sashimi-grade tuna, chopped avocado in place of the watermelon, and freshly chopped cilantro leaves in place of the green onion.

shrimp chipotle ceviche
Prepare the basic recipe, using 8 raw, peeled, and deveined medium-sized shrimp, cut into 1/2-inch pieces, in place of the fish; 2 chipotle canned chiles in adobo sauce, chopped, in place of the watermelon; and freshly chopped cilantro in place of the onion.

lobster, poblano & mango ceviche
Prepare the basic recipe, using 4 fresh or frozen and thawed lobster tails—cooked in boiling water for 3 minutes or until the shells turn red, and then chopped—in place of the fish; 2 pitted and chopped mangoes in place of the watermelon; 1 poblano chile—roasted, stemmed, seeded, and chopped—in place of the tomatoes; and freshly chopped cilantro in place of the onion.

variations

snapper aotearoa

see base recipe page 35

samoan snapper
Prepare the basic recipe, using the juice of 3 fresh lemons in place of lemon and lime juice, and 1/4 cup finely chopped green onions in place of the red onion. Garnish with thin slices of lemon.

grilled snapper aotearoa
Prepare the basic recipe, but leave the snapper fillets whole. Brush with vegetable oil on each side and grill over a hot fire for about 3 1/2 minutes on each side, turning once. Stir together the citrus juices, vegetables, coconut milk, and salt to taste. Serve the fish in a pool of the sauce.

thai-style snapper
Prepare the basic recipe, replacing the 2 lemons with 1 or 2 more limes. Instead of the vegetables, stir 1 small seeded and chopped red or green serrano pepper and 1 tablespoon green curry paste with the coconut milk. Garnish with chopped fresh cilantro.

orange grove snapper
Prepare the basic recipe, using the zest and juice of 1 orange in place of the juice of 1 lime. Garnish with chopped fresh cilantro.

variations

yellowtail tartare in tortilla cones

see base recipe page 36

tartare trio
Omit tortilla cones. In place of the yellowtail, place 2 ounces finely chopped tilapia, 2 ounces finely chopped salmon, and 2 ounces finely chopped tuna in each of 3 glass or ceramic bowls. Combine remaining ingredients, then divide among the 3 bowls of fish. Cover and chill from 1 to 24 hours, then drain off excess liquid. Place a mound of each tartare on each plate and garnish with fresh chopped cilantro.

salmon tartare
Prepare basic recipe, replacing flour tortillas with green jalapeño-flavored tortillas and yellowtail with salmon.

bay scallop tartare
Prepare basic recipe, replacing flour tortillas with red chile-flavored tortillas and yellowtail with 4 ounces small bay scallops.

tartare tower
Prepare the basic recipe, omitting the tortilla cones. Spoon the tartare into 4–6 ramekins; cover and chill up to 24 hours. To serve, drain off excess liquid from each ramekin. Carefully invert in the center of each plate. Drizzle Mango & Lime Salsa (page 265) around the perimeter of each plate, and garnish with chopped cilantro.

all steamed up

Since Neolithic times, simple steaming, poaching, and boiling have been favored cooking methods for fish and seafood. For a moist, succulent result, cook just until the fish is opaque or the shellfish has turned pale pink. Add color and texture with a variety of classic sauces from around the world.

classic shrimp cocktail

see variations page 64

To take a shrimp cocktail from ho-hum to wow involves just a little more work on the part of the cook. Get the best flavor by starting with whole, head-on shrimp and cook them yourself. Mix up classic cocktail sauce in a few seconds, then serve it all chilled.

4 cups water
1/4 cup kosher or table salt
1 lb. large (21–30 count) shrimp, deveined,
    shell on, with heads intact, rinsed, and
    patted dry
crisp lettuce leaves, to serve

for the classic cocktail sauce
1 cup tomato ketchup
prepared horseradish to taste
fresh lemon juice to taste
bottled hot sauce to taste

Bring a large pot of salted water to a boil. Add the shrimp. Cover and cook for 6–8 minutes or until the shrimp are pink and just opaque. Check periodically and do not overcook. Remove from the cooking water and let stand in very cold water to stop the cooking. When cool enough to handle, twist off the head and pull off the legs of each shrimp. Hold the tail and lift the shell upward to peel. Use a small knife to remove the black vein (the digestive tract). Rinse under cold water, then cover and chill until ready to serve.

Whisk the cocktail sauce ingredients together in a small bowl. Cover and refrigerate until ready to serve. To serve, arrange crisp lettuce leaves on each plate or in a cocktail glass. Top with shrimp and cocktail sauce.

Serves 4

steamed crab

see variations page 65

Live crabs steamed in a flavorful liquid can be picked and eaten with melted butter right then and there. The picked meat can also be used in lump form in salads or crab cakes; flaked crabmeat is more suitable for dips and fillings. While it's easy to steam crab, it's more difficult to pick out the meat—that's why crabmeat is expensive to buy already picked. But once you get the hang of it, you're fine.

1 dozen live crabs
1 cup cider vinegar
1 cup beer

3 tbsp. kosher or sea salt
1 tbsp. Old Bay or Zatarain's seasoning or other
   crab boil seasoning

Make sure that all the crabs are alive; discard any that do not move. Bring the vinegar, beer, salt, and seasoning to a boil in a large steamer (or a pot with a wire rack placed in the bottom to keep crabs from touching the boiling water). Cover, reduce heat to simmer, and steam for 20–25 minutes or until all the crabs are bright orange. Transfer the crabs to a newspaper-covered flat surface. Have ready a bowl for the crabmeat, a bowl for the good shells, and a trash can. When cool enough to handle, take one crab and turn it smooth shell-side down. Pull off the legs and claws; set them aside. Pull off the narrow and pointy (male crab) or wide, triangular (female) plate. Turn the crab on its side. Wedge your thumbs between the smooth shell and the body and pull apart. Remove anything that is not fine, white crabmeat. Break the body in half and pick out the crabmeat. Crack the claws and legs with pliers and extract more meat. Save the larger shells to make shellfish stock. Serve the picked crab with melted butter.

Serves 4

mussels steamed in white wine, garlic & herbs

see variations page 66

One of the classic dishes of Belgium served with frites and homemade mayonnaise, steamed mussels are easy to make and delicious to eat. Make sure you scrub away the "beard" from each mussel. Discard any that are open before you steam them and any that don't open after steaming.

1 tbsp. olive oil
1 medium onion, chopped
2 cloves garlic, thinly sliced
1 cup dry white wine

1 tbsp. chopped fresh tarragon
3 lbs. mussels, scrubbed, with beards removed
1/4 cup chopped fresh Italian parsley, to garnish

Place the oil in a large pot and sauté the onion and garlic over medium-high heat until transparent, about 4 minutes. Pour in the wine, add the tarragon, and heat to boiling. Add the mussels, cover, and cook for 5–7 minutes or until the shells open, shaking the pot occasionally. Discard any unopened mussels. To serve, ladle the mussels and their broth into 6 large soup bowls and garnish with parsley.

Serves 6

thai seafood & vegetable wraps

see variations page 67

Colorful, delicious, and easy to make, these see-through wraps show off the ingredients. Serve with a dipping sauce for appetizers or a light lunch.

1/4 cup soy sauce
1 tbsp. honey
1 tsp. toasted sesame oil
1/2 tsp. black sesame seeds
1 clove garlic, minced
2 oz. rice sticks
8 oz. peeled and deveined cooked shrimp, coarsely chopped (about 1 1/2 cups)

1/4 cup unseasoned rice wine vinegar
1 1/2 tsp. grated fresh gingerroot
1/2 cup grated carrots
1/4 cup chopped fresh mint
2 green onions, thinly sliced
8 (8 1/2-inch) rice paper wraps
1 cup shredded romaine lettuce

Whisk the soy sauce, honey, sesame oil, sesame seeds, and minced garlic together in a small bowl. Cook the rice sticks in enough boiling water to cover for 2–3 minutes or until tender. Drain and rinse with cold water. Drain again and snap rice sticks into bite-sized pieces. In a small bowl, combine the shrimp, vinegar, and gingerroot. In another bowl, combine the carrots, mint, and green onions.

Dip one rice paper wrap at a time into a shallow bowl of warm water. Shake off extra water and lay flat between clean, damp kitchen towels. Let stand for 3–4 minutes or until pliable. Lay out each rice paper wrapper on a flat surface. Layer lettuce, rice sticks, shrimp mixture, and carrot mixture. Carefully roll up into a cylinder, folding in the sides as you go. Cut the wraps in half on the diagonal and serve with the dipping sauce.

Serves 8

singapore-style steamed fish in banana leaves

see variations page 68

Wrapping fish and its flavorings in banana leaves, then steaming, produces a tender, aromatic result. Fish fillets steam the quickest, but you can also do this with small, whole, cleaned fish—just allow 15 or 20 minutes more. You can buy frozen banana leaves in packages at Hispanic markets or in some supermarkets. Just thaw, cut to size, and wrap the fish. If you can't find banana leaves, you can use aluminum foil.

1/2 cup desiccated (not sweetened, flaked)
   coconut
3/4 cup hot water
1 clove garlic
1 tbsp. freshly grated ginger
1/4 tsp. ground gingerroot
1 tsp. ground coriander

1 tsp. garam masala or curry powder
1 tsp. fine kosher or sea salt
1 1/2 tbsp. fresh lemon juice
1 tbsp. chopped fresh cilantro leaves
4 tilapia, cod, pomfret, or halibut fillets, skin
   removed, rinsed, and patted dry
1 large banana leaf, cut in pieces

In a food processor, process the coconut, water, garlic, fresh and ground gingerroot, coriander, garam masala, salt, and lemon juice until very finely ground. Stir in the cilantro leaves. Place each fish fillet in the center of a piece of banana leaf big enough to completely enclose it. Top the fish fillet with a fourth of the coconut mixture, then wrap up in the piece of banana leaf. Fill a steamer with water. Bring to a boil. Place the wrapped fish fillets, seam-side down, in a single layer in the steamer basket or on the rack. Cover and steam for 15 minutes or until fish begins to flake when tested with a fork in the thickest part of the fillet. Unwrap and eat.

Serves 4

chinese seafood dumplings

see variations page 69

Dumplings of all kinds help celebrate Chinese New Year, usually in February. But these are delicious any time and great for appetizers or dim sum. This recipe makes several dozen dumplings, but they'll all be gone in a hurry. You can use either fresh or frozen raw shrimp.

1 lb. medium raw shrimp (31–35 count), peeled and deveined, rinsed, and patted dry
2 green onions, coarsely chopped
1 tbsp. coarsely chopped fresh cilantro
1 tbsp. coarsely chopped fresh mint
2 tsp. soy sauce
fine kosher or sea salt to taste
2 tbsp. heavy cream

54 (3 1/2-inch diameter) round dumpling wrappers, gyoza skins, or pot sticker wrappers
1 large egg, beaten with 2 tbsp. water
Asian Vinaigrette (page 27), Miso-Soy Sauce (page 38), and/or Garlic-Soy Sauce (page 41) for dipping

In a food processor, pulse the shrimp, green onions, cilantro, mint, and soy sauce together until finely chopped. Season to taste. Transfer the mixture to a bowl and stir in the cream. Arrange the wrappers on a flat surface. Brush the egg mixture around the perimeter of each wrapper. Place a rounded teaspoon of filling in the center, then fold wrapper into a half-moon shape and press the edges together to seal.

Bring a large saucepan of water to a boil. Add the dumplings in batches, and cook until the skins turn transparent and the shrimp bits are pink, about 2 minutes. Drain in a colander and serve warm with a dipping sauce.

Serves 8–10

classic poached salmon

see variations page 70

Pale coral-colored poached salmon on a platter is delicious for a breakfast, brunch, lunch, dinner, or a festive meal of little plates. Hollandaise (page 264) is the classic sauce to serve with it, but many other sauces are also delicious accompaniments.

2 lbs. salmon fillet, skin on and any bones
    removed, rinsed, and patted dry
fine kosher or sea salt
ground white pepper
lemon slices, watercress, and cucumber slices,
    to garnish

for the court bouillon
12 cups (3 quarts) water
1 cup dry white wine
1/2 cup tarragon vinegar
2 cups chopped carrots
2 cups chopped onions
6 fresh parsley stalks
2 bay leaves
1 tbsp. whole black peppercorns

Preheat the oven to 450°F. Season the salmon fillet, wrap in a double layer of cheesecloth, and place in a large buttered baking dish. Bring the 3 quarts of water to a boil in a large pot, then stir in the wine, vinegar, carrots, onions, parsley stalks, bay leaves, and peppercorns. Simmer for 15 minutes. Carefully pour the court bouillon over the salmon so it reaches three-fourths of the way up the fillet. Poach in the oven for 7–8 minutes. Remove from the oven and let salmon cool in the broth. When cool enough to handle, remove salmon from the broth, remove cheesecloth from the salmon, and place the salmon on a serving platter. Garnish with lemon and cucumber slices and watercress sprigs. Serve warm or cover and chill to serve later. Strain the court bouillon, let cool to room temperature, then freeze for another use.

Serves 4

butter-poached lobster

see variations page 71

Butter poaching is a gentle way to get the maximum flavor from previously frozen (cooked and thawed) seafood. The poaching liquid can then be flavored with a variety of ingredients to make interesting sauces.

8 small frozen and thawed rock lobster tails
and/or claws
lemon juice to taste
kosher or sea salt and ground white pepper to
taste
4 tbsp. sweet butter

1/4 cup chicken stock, shellfish stock (page 65)
or court bouillon (page 58)
1/4 cup dry white wine
1/4 cup dry white vermouth, port, or sherry
1/4 cup heavy cream

Preheat oven to 400°F. Gently remove the lobster meat from the shell to keep it all in one piece. Drizzle with lemon juice and season with salt and white pepper. Heat the butter in a heavy casserole (with a lid) until bubbling. Quickly roll the lobster meat in the hot butter, then top the casserole with a parchment paper round, cover with the lid, and place in the oven for 6–8 minutes or until lobster meat is white and springy to the touch.

Remove casserole from the oven. Transfer the lobster to a platter and keep warm. Place the casserole over high heat and stir in the stock and white wine. Reduce until the liquid is syrupy, about 5 minutes. Whisk in the vermouth and bring to a boil. Cook for 1 minute. Whisk in the cream. Taste for seasoning, and serve the sauce over the lobster.

Serves 4

easy paella

see variations page 72

Paella is a great party dish and this version takes only about 45 minutes to prepare.

2 tbsp. olive oil
1 cup chopped onion
1/2 cup chopped red bell pepper
1/2 cup chopped green bell pepper
4 garlic cloves, minced
1 bay leaf
2 cups chopped canned tomatoes, with juices
1/2 tsp. saffron threads or 1 tbsp. paprika
2 cups short-grain, risotto, or paella rice

5 cups chicken broth or court bouillon
   (page 58)
8 Manila or littleneck clams, scrubbed
8 mussels, scrubbed, beards removed
8 peeled and deveined large raw shrimp, rinsed
   and patted dry
1 cup frozen peas, thawed
chopped fresh Italian parsley, to garnish

Heat the olive oil in a large paella pan or large pot. Sauté the onion, peppers, and garlic over medium-high heat until softened, about 5 minutes. Add the bay leaf, tomatoes, saffron, and rice, and cook, stirring, for 2 minutes. Add the chicken broth and bring to a boil. Reduce the heat, cover, and simmer for 15–20 minutes or until the rice is almost tender. Add the clams, mussels, and shrimp, cover, and simmer for 10 minutes or until the clams and mussels have opened and the shrimp are pink and opaque. Stir in the peas until warmed through. Serve garnished with Italian parsley.

Serves 8

seashore lobster dinner

see variations page 73

This one-pot meal—cooked outdoors over a driftwood fire or indoors on the stovetop—conjures up summers at the seaside. Spread layers of newspapers over the table for the traditional (and easy) clean-up. Dump the contents of the pot in the middle of the table and it's all hands on deck.

4 live (1-lb.) lobsters
1 lb. trimmed string beans

4 ears shucked corn
Sesame Mayonnaise (page 275)

Bring a large pot of salted water to a boil. Add the lobsters, cover, and cook for 8 minutes or until starting to turn red in places. Add the string beans and corn and cook, covered, until the beans are almost crisp-tender and the lobsters have turned completely red, about 4 more minutes. Drain the pot and dump the contents on a newspaper-covered table. Serve with Sesame Mayonnaise.

Serves 4

variations

classic shrimp cocktail

see base recipe page 49

simple boiled crawfish
Prepare basic recipe, using crawfish in place of shrimp and adding Cajun seasoning to taste to cocktail sauce. Before cooking, soak the live crawfish in a mixture of 4 cups cold water and 1 cup salt for 2 hours so they expel any mud. Drain and rinse before boiling.

smoked shrimp cocktail
Prepare an indirect fire in a grill. Make an aluminum foil packet, place 1 cup dry wood chips in it, close packet, and poke several holes in top. Place packet on the coals or near a gas jet. Arrange shrimp in a disposable foil pan, brush with olive oil, and place on indirect (no heat) side. At the first wisp of smoke, close grill. Smoke shrimp for 30 minutes or until pink and almost opaque. Proceed with recipe.

classic shrimp cocktail with mango lime sauce
Prepare basic recipe, using Mango & Lime Salsa (page 265) in place of cocktail sauce.

crab cocktail
Prepare basic recipe, using crabmeat in place of shrimp.

variations

steamed crab

see base recipe page 50

steamed lobster
Prepare basic recipe, using 4 live lobsters instead of crab. Steam for 20–25 minutes or until they turn red. Pick apart like crab and serve with melted butter.

shellfish stock
Roast 4–6 cups of steamed, cracked crab, shrimp, or lobster shells on cookie sheet for 10 minutes at 400°F. Put shells in large pot, cover with water, bring to a simmer. For 20 minutes, skim away foam on surface. Add 1 cup dry white wine, 1 chopped onion, 1 cup chopped celery, 1 cup chopped carrot, 1 bay leaf, 1 tablespoon tomato paste, and 1 teaspoon dried thyme. For 30 minutes, skim off foam. Remove from heat; strain through double layers of cheesecloth. Do not press on shells. Discard solids. Season to taste. Freeze in 2-cup measures. Makes 2 quarts.

easy crab salad
Combine 1 1/2 cups lump crabmeat with 1 tablespoon Dijon mustard, 1/2 cup mayonnaise, 1 tablespoon fresh dill weed, salt, and white pepper. Serve chilled.

steamed crab with ginger-lime sauce
Prepare basic recipe, using Ginger-Lime Sauce (page 39) in place of melted butter.

variations

mussels steamed in white wine, garlic & herbs

see base recipe page 53

mussels steamed in white wine & saffron

Prepare basic recipe, using 1/2 teaspoon saffron threads in place of tarragon.

mussels steamed in beer

Prepare basic recipe, using 1 (12-ounce) bottle of beer in place of wine and tarragon.

steamed clams with casino butter

Prepare basic recipe, using cherrystone, littleneck, or steamer clams in place of mussels. To make Casino Butter, mix 4 strips crisp and crumbled bacon, 8 tablespoons softened butter, 1/4 cup finely chopped green onions, bottled hot sauce to taste, 1 teaspoon Worcestershire sauce, 1/4 cup fresh lemon juice, salt, and pepper. Toast slices of French bread. Serve each bowl of clams with slices of bread and Casino Butter.

sake-steamed clams

Prepare the basic recipe, using cherrystone, littleneck, or steamer clams in place of mussels. In place of wine, garlic, and herbs, use 1/2 cup sake, 1/2 cup mirin, and 1 tablespoon unseasoned rice vinegar. Cover and steam clams until opened, then transfer to bowls. Stir 2 chopped green onions, 2 tablespoons soy sauce, and 6 tablespoons butter into steaming liquid, then ladle liquid over clams.

thai seafood & vegetable wraps

see base recipe page 54

thai fish & vegetable wraps
Prepare basic recipe, using 1 1/2 cups cooked fish in place of shrimp.

thai seafood & vegetable wraps with two sauces
Prepare basic recipe, using salmon in place of shrimp and adding Mango &
Lime Salsa (page 265) as another dipping sauce.

baja seafood & vegetable wraps
Prepare basic recipe, using 10-inch flour tortillas in place of rice paper
wraps, 1 chopped avocado in place of rice sticks, 1 tablespoon bottled
chipotle sauce in place of fresh gingerroot, and cilantro in place of mint.
Serve with more bottled chipotle sauce in place of dipping sauce.

indonesian shrimp & peanut wraps with papaya lime sauce
Combine cooked shrimp, gingerroot, and green onion. Instead of rice sticks,
carrots, and mint, stir in 1/2 cup finely chopped salted roasted peanuts, 1
tablespoon fish sauce, 2 tablespoons sweet chili sauce, and 1/4 cup chopped
cilantro. Stir in the romaine. Spoon mixture onto each rice paper wrap and
roll up. Add Papaya & Lime Salsa (page 277) as a dipping sauce.

variations

singapore-style steamed fish in banana leaves

see base recipe page 56

singapore-style baked fish in banana leaves
Prepare basic recipe, but instead of steaming, bake fish on a cookie sheet at 350°F for 15 minutes.

rainforest fish in banana leaves
Prepare basic recipe, using farm-raised catfish in place of tilapia, ground chipotle in place of garam masala, and fresh lime juice in place of lemon. Omit fresh and ground gingerroot.

chinese-style fish steamed in banana leaves
Lightly brush fillets with toasted sesame oil and top with 1/2 cup chopped mushrooms. Drizzle with 1 tablespoon soy sauce. Sprinkle with 2 chopped green onions and 2 tablespoons chopped fresh cilantro. Wrap in banana leaves and proceed with recipe.

plated perch
Butter inside of a large heatproof plate and arrange lake perch fillets on it in a single layer. Sprinkle with salt and ground white pepper and drizzle with 2 tablespoons each dry white wine and fresh lemon juice. Invert a second buttered plate over fish. Place plated fish over a pan of boiling water and steam for 15 minutes.

chinese seafood dumplings

see base recipe page 57

chinese crabmeat dumplings
Prepare basic recipe, using 1 pound lump crabmeat in place of shrimp.

seafood wontons
Prepare basic recipe, using wonton wrappers in place of dumpling wrappers. Moisten the perimeter of each wrapper with the egg mixture, fold the wrapper over the filling to form a triangle, and press the edges together to seal. Fry in hot oil, in batches, until golden brown.

crab rangoon
Instead of basic recipe, make Crab Rangoon in wonton wrappers. In food processor, pulse 8 ounces cream cheese; 8 ounces cooked crabmeat, drained and flaked; 1/2 teaspoon Worcestershire sauce; 1/2 teaspoon soy sauce; 2 finely chopped green onions; 1 minced garlic clove; and ground white pepper to taste. Moisten the perimeter of wonton wrappers with diluted egg, fold wrapper over filling to form a triangle, and press edges together to seal. Fry in hot oil, in batches, until golden brown.

chinese salmon dumplings
Prepare the basic recipe, using raw salmon in place of shrimp.

variations

classic poached salmon

see base recipe page 58

poached halibut
Prepare basic recipe, using halibut in place of salmon.

poached salmon aïoli platter
Prepare basic recipe. Serve salmon on a platter, surrounded by cured black olives, artichoke hearts, baby carrots, steamed thin string beans, and cherry tomatoes. Serve Aïoli (page 262) on the side.

traditional aïoli platter
Prepare basic recipe, using dried, salted cod in place of salmon. Three days before poaching, soak salted cod in water. Cover and refrigerate. Each day, drain off salty water, add fresh cold water, cover, and refrigerate. When the cod is firm but rehydrated, proceed with recipe. Serve the cod on a platter as in the variation above.

classic cold poached salmon with herbed tomato vinaigrette
Prepare basic recipe. Place poached salmon on a platter, cover, and chill. Serve with Herbed Tomato Vinaigrette (page 258).

butter-poached lobster

see base recipe page 60

butter-poached shrimp
Prepare basic recipe, using raw shrimp in place of lobster and poaching 3–4 minutes until shrimp are opaque and pink.

butter-poached lobster with blood orange sauce
Prepare basic recipe, omitting vermouth and cream. When the lobster is done, carefully transfer to 4 plates. Place the pan over high heat and cook until the butter begins to brown. Remove from heat and stir in 2 tablespoons fresh blood orange juice. Pour the sauce over the lobster and serve.

butter-poached fish fillets with pernod butter sauce
Follow directions of variation above, using Pernod instead of blood orange juice.

butter-poached fish steaks
Prepare basic recipe, using fish steaks in place of lobsters. Poach for 6–8 minutes or until opaque all the way through and springy to the touch.

variations

easy paella

see base recipe page 61

cartagena–style paella

Prepare the basic recipe, adding 8 bone-in chicken thighs. Brown the chicken in the olive oil before sautéing the vegetables, then remove from the pot. Return the chicken to the pan after the rice goes in and proceed with the recipe.

puerto rican paella

Prepare the basic recipe, adding 8 previously browned bone-in chicken thighs and 1 tablespoon Sazon seasoning with the saffron. Proceed with the recipe. Stir in 1/2 cup chopped, pimento-stuffed olives with the peas and garnish with chopped fresh cilantro in place of parsley.

peruvian shrimp & almond paella

Prepare the basic recipe, using all shrimp. Just before serving, sprinkle 1/2 cup toasted, slivered almonds over the paella and fluff with a fork.

sonoran paella

Prepare the basic recipe, brown 2 links of chorizo, sliced, in the olive oil before sautéing the vegetables, then remove from the pot. Return the chorizo to the pan after the rice goes in and proceed with the recipe.

variations

seashore lobster dinner

see base recipe page 62

clam bake

Instead of basic recipe, cook 1 pound small new potatoes in a large pot of water until they can almost be pierced with a fork. Then add 4 pounds cherrystone clams and 4 ears shucked corn. Cover and cook until clams open. Serve with melted butter.

frogmore stew

Prepare basic recipe, using headless, deveined shrimp in place of lobster and adding 1 bottle of beer and 1 1/2 tablespoons Old Bay or Zatarain's crab boil seasoning to the water. Cook beans first, until almost tender. Then add shrimp and corn. Cover and cook until shrimp are pink and opaque.

soul succotash

Prepare basic recipe, using headless, deveined shrimp in place of lobster and adding 2 bottles of beer to the water. Cook beans first, until almost tender. Then add shrimp, corn, and 1 pound sliced smoked sausage. Cover and cook until shrimp are pink and opaque.

crab boil

Prepare basic recipe, using live crabs in place of lobster and 1 1/2 tablespoons Old Bay or Zatarain's crab boil seasoning to the water. Serve with melted butter instead of Sesame Mayonnaise.

simmered

From the famous bouillabaisse from the south of France, to the clam chowders of New England and the exotic coconut-and-curry-enriched soups of southeast Asia, a slowly simmered fish soup or stew can be a meal in itself.

provençal fish soup with rouille

see variations page 90

Known as bouillabaisse in Marseilles, this seafood soup has many different versions. Most contain certain ingredients—the freshest fish and shellfish, saffron, aromatic orange peel and fennel, and garlic.

1/4 cup olive oil
6 cloves garlic, minced
2 cups chopped onion
1 cup chopped bulb fennel
2 cups canned tomatoes with their liquid
1/2 tsp. saffron threads
1 tsp. grated orange zest or dried orange peel
1 tsp. dried thyme
1 lb. small, bony fish (rascasse, red mullet, drum, and/or bream), heads removed, cut into 3-inch pieces, rinsed, and patted dry

1 lb. meaty fish (John Dory, monkfish, Pacific cod, or halibut), cleaned, heads removed, cut into 3-inch pieces, rinsed, and patted dry
1 lb. shellfish, such as shell-on shrimp, clams, bay scallops, and/or langoustines
rouille (page 275)
buttered and oven-toasted slices of French bread

Heat the olive oil in a large pot over medium-high heat. Sauté the garlic, onion, and fennel until the onion is transparent, about 5 minutes. Stir in the tomatoes, saffron, orange zest, thyme, and bony and meaty fish pieces. Add enough water to cover. When the water comes to a boil again, cover and simmer for 10 minutes. Add the shellfish, bring to a simmer again, cover, and simmer for an additional 10 minutes. To serve, ladle the soup into large bowls and serve with toasted bread and rouille.

Serves 6–8

clam chowder

see variations page 91

New England-style clam chowder starts with a hearty base of salt pork or bacon, and is finished to a creamy turn.

1 slice hickory-smoked bacon, minced
1/2 tsp. butter
1 cup minced onion
1 garlic clove, minced
1/2 tsp. each: dried parsley, dill weed, basil,
    tarragon, and rosemary

1 (6.5-oz) can clams with juice
1 tbsp. all-purpose flour
1 1/2 cups half-and-half or light cream
1/4 tsp. ground white pepper
2 medium potatoes, boiled, peeled, and diced

In a large pot, sauté the bacon, butter, onion, garlic, and dried herbs over low heat. Do not allow to brown. Drain clams and set aside, reserving the juice. Slowly stir the flour and clam juices into the sauté mixture. Bring to a boil; reduce heat. Add cream and simmer 20 minutes. Add white pepper, potatoes, and clams. Heat to serving temperature, but do not boil, as this toughens the clams. Serve at once with crackers.

Serves 4

classic lobster bisque

see variations page 92

Long a dish signifying fine dining, lobster bisque takes time to make, but the rich flavor is well worth the effort.

2 (1-lb.) steamed lobsters (page 62)
1/2 cup onion, diced
1/4 cup celery, diced
1/4 cup carrot, diced
2 bay leaves
4 tbsp. butter

3 tbsp. all-purpose flour
2 cups heavy cream
1/2 cup dry sherry
1/4 cup brandy
fine kosher or sea salt and white pepper,
    to taste

Extract the lobster meat, chop, and set aside. Place the lobster shells in a roasting pan with the onion, celery, carrot, bay leaves, and butter. Roast in a preheated 400°F oven, stirring occasionally, for 45 minutes or until the lobster shells and vegetables have browned.

Remove from the oven and strain off the butter into a heavy saucepan. Place the remaining contents of the roasting pan in a large pot. Add 2 quarts water and boil until the liquid is reduced by half, about 20 minutes. Strain the stock and discard the solids.

Heat the butter in the saucepan over medium heat. Whisk in the flour and cook the roux for 2 minutes, stirring constantly, until the roux has a nutty aroma. Whisk in the lobster stock and blend well. Then add the cream, sherry, and brandy. Simmer for 30 minutes. Season to taste with salt and white pepper. Strain the bisque and stir in the lobster meat until warmed through. Serve hot.

Serves 4

thai lemongrass shrimp soup

see variations page 93

Known as tom yum goong, this popular soup gets its sour flavor from both the lemongrass and kaffir lime leaves. Both ingredients—plus fresh galangal and tamarind paste—are available at better grocery stores or Asian markets and can be frozen for future use.

6 cups water

2 (8-inch) lemongrass stalks, root end trimmed, smashed with side of chef's knife, and cut into 1-inch pieces

3 slices fresh galangal, smashed with side of chef's knife

3-4 fresh or frozen kaffir lime leaves

1 tbsp. tamarind paste

1 tbsp. bottled Asian fish sauce (nam pla)

12 small Thai chiles or 2 jalapeños, trimmed, seeded, and thinly sliced on diagonal

2 green onions, thinly sliced on diagonal

2 tbsp. roasted chile paste (nam prik pao) or tom yum paste

3/4 lb. raw shrimp, peeled and deveined

juice of 1 lime

fresh cilantro sprigs, to garnish

Bring the water to a boil in a large saucepan. Add the lemongrass, galangal, kaffir lime leaves, and tamarind paste. Bring to a boil and stir in the fish sauce, chiles, onions, roasted chile paste, and shrimp. Cover and simmer for 5 minutes or until the shrimp are pink and opaque. Remove from the heat and stir in the lime juice. Serve hot, garnished with cilantro.

Serves 4

chinese seafood soup

see variations page 94

Chopsticks or spoon? You'll need both for this hearty, flavorful soup.

1 tsp. canola oil
4 cloves garlic, finely chopped
3 cups thinly sliced Chinese or napa cabbage
1 small red Thai or serrano chile, seeded and
    thinly sliced on diagonal
4 cups chicken stock

3 tbsp. soy sauce
2 tbsp. unseasoned rice wine vinegar
1/2 lb. Chinese wheat noodles or linguine
6 oz. small raw shrimp, peeled and deveined
6 oz. bay scallops
4 green onions, thinly sliced, to garnish

In a large pot, heat the oil over medium-high heat, and sauté the garlic, cabbage, and chile until the cabbage has wilted, about 2 minutes. Stir in the chicken stock, soy sauce, and rice vinegar. Bring to a boil and add the noodles. Cook, covered, until the noodles are almost tender, about 2 minutes. Add the shrimp and scallops, cover, and simmer for 2–3 minutes or until the shrimp are pink and opaque and the scallops are white and opaque. Serve the soup garnished with green onions.

Serves 4

kerala fish curry

see variations page 95

The cuisine of Kerala, on the Malabar coast of southeastern India, combines subtropical foods with spices brought by Arab traders long ago. Known as fish aviyal, this easy curry is most aromatic served with Coconut Rice (page 270).

1/2 tsp. tamarind concentrate dissolved in
    2 tbsp. hot water
1 1/2 cups desiccated (not sweetened, flaked)
    coconut
1/4 cup finely chopped onion
1 tsp. ground cumin
1/4 tsp. ground coriander
1/4 tsp. ground red pepper
1/4 tsp. ground turmeric
1 1/2 tsp. fine kosher or sea salt

1 1/2 cups water
1/2 cup canned coconut milk
1 serrano or Thai green chile, seeded and split
    lengthwise
1 lb. pomfret, flounder, sole, or snapper fillets,
    rinsed and patted dry, and cut into 2-inch
    pieces
10 curry leaves or 4 bay leaves
1 tbsp. vegetable oil

In a food processor, blend the tamarind water, coconut, onion, cumin, coriander, red pepper, turmeric, salt, water, and coconut milk until somewhat smooth. Transfer coconut mixture to a large, deep skillet with a lid. Place the split chile in the center and heat to a simmer. Add the fish pieces in one layer, cover, and simmer for 10 minutes or until the fish is opaque. Add curry leaves and oil. Simmer for 1 minute more and serve.

Serves 8

oyster stew

see variations page 96

For many families, oyster stew is a dish served on a meatless Christmas Eve or other holiday. For the best flavor and texture, gently simmer the oysters for only a few minutes, so they do not become too tough.

1 cup finely chopped leeks
1 cup finely chopped onions
2 tbsp. butter
5 dozen shucked oysters, liquor reserved
4 cups chicken stock

1 bay leaf
1/2 tsp. dried summer savory
2 cups peeled and diced baking potatoes
4 cups heavy cream
snipped fresh chives, to garnish

In a large pot, sauté the leeks and onions in butter until transparent, about 4 minutes. Stir in the reserved oyster liquor, chicken stock, bay leaf, summer savory, and potatoes. Bring to a boil and cook until the potatoes are tender, about 15 minutes. Puree the soup in batches, and return to the pot. Stir in the cream and bring to a boil. Reduce the heat, add the shucked oysters, cover, and simmer for 4 minutes or until the oysters are just firm. Serve garnished with snipped chives.

Serves 6–8

red snapper veracruzano

see variations page 97

This Mexican classic from the Gulf of Mexico gets its distinctive flavor from both fresh and brined ingredients. Another plus—it's ready in minutes and perfect with a chilled Mexican beer.

2 tbsp. canola oil
1 large onion, thinly sliced
4 garlic cloves, minced
2 tbsp. chopped pickled jalapeños
3 plum tomatoes, seeded and chopped
1 cup water
1/2 cup pimento-stuffed green olives, chopped

1 tbsp. fresh or 1 tsp. dried oregano
4 (6-oz.) red snapper, mahi mahi, tilapia, or halibut fillets, rinsed and patted dry
coarse kosher or sea salt and ground black pepper
lime wedges, to garnish

Heat the oil in a large skillet over medium-high heat and sauté the onion until golden, about 4–6 minutes. Stir in the garlic and jalapeños and cook another minute. Add tomatoes and 1 cup water and cook, stirring, until almost evaporated, about 6–8 minutes. Stir in the olives and oregano. Arrange the fish over the vegetables, cover, and simmer for 7 minutes or until the fish is opaque. Season to taste and serve garnished with lime wedges.

Serves 4

seafood zarzuela

see variations page 98

In Mexico, "zarzuela" means a three-act operetta that alternates between singing and speaking parts. It has given its name to this delicious, three-step dish that features fish and shellfish from both the Gulf and Pacific Coasts of Mexico.

1/2 cup vegetable oil
2 cups chopped onions
1/2 cup chopped fresh Italian parsley
1 cup long- or short-grain rice
1 (15-oz.) can chopped tomatoes with liquid
1 cup bottled clam juice
1 cup water

1/4 cup chopped fresh cilantro
1 lb. halibut, grouper, or monkfish fillets, rinsed
    and patted dry, cut into 1-inch pieces
1/2 lb. small bay scallops
1/2 lb. raw large shrimp, peeled and deveined
fresh avocado slices and lime wedges,
    to garnish

Heat the oil in a large pot over medium-high heat. Sauté the onions, stirring, until transparent, about 5 minutes. Stir in the parsley and rice and cook, stirring, until the rice begins to brown. Stir in the tomatoes, clam juice, and water. Bring to a boil, then reduce the heat, cover, and simmer for 15 minutes. Reduce the heat to low and stir in the cilantro, fish, scallops, and shrimp. Cover and cook for 10 minutes or until fish and shellfish are opaque. Serve in bowls, garnished with avocado slices and lime wedges.

Serves 4

singaporean laksa

see variations page 99

A fusion of Chinese and Malay cuisine, this spicy rice noodle soup is a popular street food in Indonesia and China. "Laksa," a word meaning 10,000, indicates that the flavoring base has lots of different parts. There are many varieties of laksas, but all are based on noodles cooked in a spicy broth, and are rich and creamy.

for the laksa paste
2 tbsp. vegetable oil
1/2 tsp. ground turmeric
1 inch fresh gingerroot, grated
1 lemongrass stalk, root end trimmed, mashed
    with the flat end of a chef's knife, and cut
    into 1-inch pieces
3 garlic cloves, minced
2 small Thai or serrano chiles, seeded
    and chopped
2 tbsp. vegetable oil

12 raw jumbo shrimp or large tiger or king
    shrimp, peeled, shells and heads reserved
4 cups water
1/2 cup dry white wine
1 cup finely chopped onions
2 kaffir lime leaves, fresh or frozen
2 cups chicken or fish stock
1 tbsp. soy sauce
12 oz. fine dry rice noodles or vermicelli, cooked
    according to package directions
2 dozen fresh mussels, scrubbed and debearded
chopped fresh cilantro leaves and green onions,
    to garnish

Puree the laksa ingredients together in a food processor or mortar and pestle until smooth. For the soup, heat 2 tablespoons oil in a large soup pot and sauté the shrimp shells and heads until bright pink. Add the water and wine and bring to a boil. Cook until reduced by half, about 8 minutes. Strain and reserve the stock; discard the solids. Heat 2 more tablespoons oil in the pot and sauté the onions until transparent, about 4 minutes.

Stir in the laksa paste until well blended. Add the reserved shrimp stock, kaffir lime leaves, chicken or fish stock, and soy sauce. Bring to a boil. Add the cooked noodles and mussels, cover, and simmer for 1 minute. Add the shrimp, cover, and simmer for 2–3 minutes or until the shrimp are pink and opaque and the mussels have opened. Serve in bowls, garnished with cilantro and green onions.

Serves 6

variations

provençal fish soup with rouille

see base recipe page 75

provençal fish soup marseillaise
Prepare basic recipe. To serve, ladle broth into bowls and serve with toasted bread and rouille. Arrange cooked fish, shellfish, and vegetables on platter as a second course with Aïoli (page 262).

cap d'antibes-style fish soup
Prepare basic recipe, adding 1 extra cup chopped bulb fennel and 1 pound small new potatoes to vegetables.

parisian-style fish soup
Prepare basic recipe, omitting shellfish and adding 1 extra pound fish and 1 bay leaf. When fish and vegetables are cooked, pass soup, in batches, through a food mill. Discard solids. Return brothy puree to the pot, bring to a boil, then strain through a sieve. Serve with toasted bread and rouille.

new orleans-style fish soup
Prepare basic recipe, adding 1 cup chopped celery to onions and garlic. Use redfish or red snapper for the fish and shrimp for the shellfish. Add 2 teaspoons filé powder or 1 bay leaf and 1 cup dry white wine to the water.

clam chowder

see base recipe page 76

manhattan-style clam chowder
Prepare the basic recipe, omitting the flour and half-and-half. Add
1 (14.5-ounce) can chopped tomatoes with their juice to the clam juices
and proceed with the recipe.

mussel chowder
Prepare the basic recipe, omitting the clams and clam juice and using 1 slice
more of minced bacon. While the vegetables and half-and-half are simmering,
steam 2 pounds scrubbed mussels in 2 cups wine until shells open. Remove
the mussels from their shells, strain the cooking liquid through a paper towel,
and add the mussels and strained liquid to the pot. Proceed with the recipe.

chaudrée
Prepare the basic recipe, using 1 pound fresh squid—body only, cut into fine
strips—in place of clams, omitting clam juice, and adding 2 cups dry white
wine to the cooking liquid. Proceed with the recipe and cook until squid
are opaque.

clam & corn chowder
Prepare the basic recipe, adding 1 cup yellow kernel corn with the potatoes.
Garnish with chopped Italian parsley.

variations

classic lobster bisque

see base recipe page 79

quick lobster bisque
Instead of basic recipe, thaw and chop 1–2 cups frozen lobster meat. Mix with the sherry and brandy. Heat 4 cups canned or frozen lobster bisque, stir in the marinated lobster, and serve hot.

easy lobster bisque
Eliminate roasting and boiling steps. Begin with 1–2 cups frozen lobster meat, thawed and chopped. Mix with the sherry and brandy; set aside. Heat 4 cups prepared Alfredo sauce in a large saucepan. Add the lobster mixture and heat through. Puree if you wish and serve hot.

crab & shrimp bisque
Follow steps for Easy Lobster Bisque above, using 1 pound cooked shrimp and 1/2 pound cooked crabmeat in place of lobster.

cold lobster bisque
Prepare the basic recipe. Let cool, then cover and refrigerate. To serve, garnish each cup with a swirl of cream and a sprinkling of chopped fresh tarragon.

thai lemongrass shrimp soup

see base recipe page 80

thai lemongrass fish soup
Prepare the basic recipe, using 12 ounces raw fish fillets, cut into 2-inch pieces, in place of shrimp.

easy thai lemongrass shrimp soup
Instead of basic recipe, bring 6 cups of water to a boil. Stir in 2 tablespoons green curry paste; 2 tablespoons fish sauce; 3 green onions sliced on the diagonal; 12 small Thai chiles or 2 jalapeños, seeded and thinly sliced on diagonal; and 12 ounces peeled and deveined shrimp. Bring to a boil, then reduce the heat and simmer until the shrimp are pink and opaque. Stir in the juice of 1 fresh lime and garnish with cilantro.

thai lemongrass scallop soup
Prepare the basic recipe, using 12 ounces bay scallops in place of shrimp.

indonesian shrimp & chile soup
Prepare the basic recipe, using 1/4 cup sambal oelek in place of roasted chile paste. Garnish with lime, chopped cilantro, and toasted peanuts.

variations

chinese seafood soup

see base recipe page 82

chinese fish soup
Prepare the basic recipe, using 12 ounces fresh fish fillet, cut into 2-inch pieces, in place of shrimp and scallops. Simmer the fish for 2–3 minutes or until opaque and firm.

japanese fish soup
Prepare the basic recipe, using 3 cups dashi soup stock and 3 tablespoons miso paste in place of the chicken stock and soy sauce.

easy asian fish soup
Prepare the basic recipe, using 4 cups prepared Asian-style shrimp broth (made from 2 shrimp-style ramen noodle packages; omit noodles) in place of the chicken stock, soy sauce, and wine vinegar.

aussie-style seafood soup
Prepare the basic recipe, using Australian banana prawns for the shrimp and Tasmanian blue mussels for the scallops.

kerala fish curry

see base recipe page 83

kerala shrimp curry
Prepare the basic recipe, using 2 pounds large raw shrimp, peeled and deveined, in place of fish.

shrimp vindaloo
Instead of the basic recipe, simmer 2 pounds large raw shrimp, peeled and deveined, in 3 cups prepared vindaloo sauce until pink and opaque. Serve over rice or with naan.

fish molee
Instead of the basic recipe, fry 2 cups sliced onion in 1 tablespoon oil until medium brown in a large, deep skillet with a lid. Add 2 cloves minced garlic, 1 teaspoon grated fresh gingerroot, 1 tablespoon ground coriander, 1/2 teaspoon ground cumin, 1/2 teaspoon ground turmeric, and 1/8 teaspoon ground red pepper. Stir in 1/4 cup water, 1 cup coconut milk, and 1 tablespoon white vinegar. Bring to a boil, then simmer. Add 1 pound boneless fish cut in 2-inch pieces, cover, and simmer until opaque.

kerala salmon curry
Prepare the basic recipe, using salmon in place of white fish.

variations

oyster stew

see base recipe page 84

oyster & sausage stew
Prepare the basic recipe, adding 8 ounces fresh pork sausage or chorizo to the leeks and onions.

belgian mussel stew
Instead of the basic recipe, sauté 1/2 cup chopped onions, 1/2 cup chopped carrots, and 1/2 cup chopped celery in 4 tablespoons butter until transparent. Whisk in 2 cups heavy cream and set aside. Steam 2 pounds scrubbed and debearded mussels in 2 cups dry white wine, covered, until mussels open, about 5 minutes. Strain mussel cooking liquid through cheesecloth, reserving mussels, and whisk into cream mixture. Add mussels, season with salt and ground white pepper, and garnish with chopped fresh Italian parsley.

vichyssoise-style oyster stew
Prepare the basic recipe, adding 2 extra cups diced potatoes.

easy oyster stew
Instead of the basic recipe, prepare canned potato soup according to directions, adding half dry white wine and half heavy cream in place of broth. Bring to a boil, add 5 dozen shucked oysters, cover, and cook until the oysters are just firm. Serve garnished with snipped chives.

red snapper veracruzano

see base recipe page 86

easy snapper veracruzano
Prepare the basic recipe, using 2 cups prepared tomato salsa in place of tomatoes and oregano.

shrimp veracruzano
Prepare the basic recipe, using 12 ounces peeled and deveined raw shrimp in place of snapper. Cover and cook until the shrimp are pink and opaque.

red snapper on a bed of mango
Prepare the basic recipe, using 2 cups chopped fresh mango in place of tomatoes. Omit the green olives and oregano. Add 1 tablespoon fresh lemon juice, 1 chopped canned chipotle in adobo sauce, and 1 teaspoon fresh lime juice to the mango mixture, then place the fish on top and proceed with the recipe.

creole snapper
Prepare the basic recipe, using drained capers in place of pickled jalapeños and 2 teaspoons creole seasoning in place of oregano.

variations

seafood zarzuela

see base recipe page 87

cilantro-saffron zarzuela
Prepare the basic recipe, adding 1 teaspoon saffron threads to the water and using fresh clams or mussels in place of fish. (Do not use any clams or mussels that have opened before cooking and discard any that do not open after cooking.)

zarzuela with squash, tomatoes & saffron
Prepare the basic recipe, adding 1 teaspoon saffron threads to the water and 1 cup diced zucchini or yellow summer squash with the seafood.

roasted poblano zarzuela
Prepare the basic recipe, adding 1 cup roasted, stemmed, seeded, and chopped poblano chile to the broth after browning the rice.

smoky chipotle zarzuela
Prepare the basic recipe, adding 1/4 cup bottled smoked chipotle sauce with the seafood.

singaporean laksa

see base recipe page 88

coconut laksa
Prepare the basic recipe, using 1 (14-ounce) can coconut milk in place of chicken stock.

cockle curry laksa
Prepare the basic recipe, using cockles in place of mussels. Serve each bowl with a spoonful of sambal chili paste to taste and chopped fresh cilantro.

lobster laksa
Prepare the basic recipe, using 2 pounds lobster in place of shrimp and mussels. Steam the lobsters first, remove the meat and cut it into small pieces, and reserve. Crack the shells, and proceed with the recipe. Add the reserved lobster meat to the soup right before serving.

katong laksa
Prepare the basic recipe, cutting the cooked rice noodles into small pieces before adding them to the soup.

into the frying pan

From beer-battered English fish 'n' chips, to the fried catfish of the Mississippi Delta and fritto misto from the Italian coast, frying makes fish and shellfish especially delectable. Fried seafood tastes great served with malt vinegar as well as tartar and jezebel sauces.

flash-fried calamari

see variations page 116

Calamari—small squid—are so easy and quick to fry, it's no wonder they're on restaurant menus around the world. They taste wonderful with almost any kind of dipping sauce, so offer two or three when you entertain.

vegetable oil for frying
1 lb. small squid, heads removed, bodies cut
    into thin rings, tentacles left whole
1 cup all-purpose flour

2 large eggs, beaten
1 cup fine dry breadcrumbs
coarse kosher or sea salt to taste
dipping sauces of your choice

Heat 1/2 inch of oil in a large skillet over medium-high heat. Rinse the calamari under cold, running water and gently pat dry. Put the flour in one bowl, the beaten eggs in a second bowl, and the breadcrumbs in a third bowl.

Toss the calamari with the flour first, then dip the calamari in the eggs, and finally in the breadcrumbs. When the oil is hot (test it with a small piece of bread or a thermometer; it should be 375°F), fry the calamari, in batches, until golden brown. Drain on paper towels and season to taste. Serve hot with dipping sauces.

Serves 4

whitefish beignets

see variations page 117

As an appetizer with a dipping sauce, as an entrée with malt vinegar, or as a sandwich filling, these crispy, tender nuggets of fish please young and old alike.

vegetable oil for frying
1 lb. whitefish fillets, rinsed and patted dry, cut
    into 4-inch pieces
1 cup all-purpose flour

1 tbsp. Cajun or Creole seasoning or barbecue
    seasoning
1 cup beer
2 large egg whites
coarse kosher or sea salt

Heat 1/2 inch of oil in a skillet set over medium-high heat. Rinse the fish under cold running water and pat dry. In a bowl, whisk together the flour, seasoning, beer, and egg whites into a batter. When the oil is hot (test it with a small piece of bread or a thermometer; it should be 375°F), dip the fish pieces in the batter, then fry in the hot oil, in batches, turning once. When golden brown, remove from the oil, drain on paper towels, and salt to taste. Serve hot.

Serves 4

crab cakes

see variations page 118

The most succulent crab cakes start with lump crabmeat, which is crabmeat in bigger pieces. Serve these with your favorite dipping sauce for appetizers, a light lunch, or atop a salad.

8 oz. fresh lump crabmeat
2/3 cup fresh breadcrumbs
1/4 cup sliced green onion
1 tbsp. Dijon mustard
1/2 tsp. dried tarragon

1/4 tsp. dried red pepper flakes
1 large egg, beaten
vegetable oil for frying

Combine the crabmeat, breadcrumbs, onion, mustard, tarragon, red pepper flakes, and egg. Shape into eight 1/2-inch-thick patties. Chill in the refrigerator for about 1/2 hour to firm up. Heat 1/2 inch of oil in a large skillet over medium-high heat. When the oil is hot (test it with a small piece of bread or a thermometer; it should be 375°F), fry the crab cakes, in batches, until golden brown, turning once. Drain on paper towels and salt to taste. Serve hot.

Serves 4

coconut prawns & jezebel sauce

see variations page 119

Add a little coconut to the batter, and you've got a crunchy, exotic, crowd-pleasing appetizer like this one, adapted from a recipe by Paul Prudhomme. These disappear fast, so make more than you think you'll need.

for the jezebel sauce
1 (10-oz.) jar orange marmalade
5 tbsp. brown mustard
5 tbsp. prepared horseradish

for the shrimp
1 tbsp. ground red pepper
1 tsp. fine kosher or sea salt
1 1/2 tsp. Hungarian paprika
1 1/2 tsp. ground black pepper
1 1/2 tsp. garlic powder
3/4 tsp. onion powder

3/4 tsp. ground dried thyme
3/4 tsp. dried oregano
1 3/4 cups all-purpose flour
1 tbsp. baking powder
2 large eggs, beaten
3/4 cup beer
3 cups desiccated (not sweetened, flaked) coconut
vegetable oil for deep-frying
4 dozen large (21–30 count) peeled and deveined raw shrimp or large prawns, tails on, rinsed, and patted dry

Stir the Jezebel Sauce ingredients together in a bowl; set aside. Combine the seasonings, flour, and baking powder in a bowl, then transfer half to a second bowl. Stir the eggs and beer into the second bowl to make a batter. Place the coconut in a third bowl. Heat the oil to a depth of 4 inches in a large saucepan or deep skillet set over medium-high heat. When the oil is hot (375°F), dredge the shrimp, in batches, in the flour mixture, then dip in the batter, then roll in the coconut. Fry in hot oil until golden. Drain on paper towels and serve with Jezebel Sauce.

Serves 12

beer-battered fish 'n' chips

see variations page 120

A classic dish from the British Isles, dating back to Victorian times, which uses tender, white-fleshed fish: cod, plaice, haddock, turbot, walleye pike, grouper, John Dory, lake perch, farm-raised catfish, tilapia, etc.

for the beer batter
1 cup all-purpose flour
1 tsp. fine kosher or sea salt
1 tsp. Hungarian paprika
1 tsp. ground fennel seed
1 tsp. ground white pepper
2 cups beer

vegetable oil for deep-frying
1 cup all-purpose flour
2 lbs. fresh white-fleshed fish fillets, rinsed and patted dry
4 large baking potatoes, peeled, and cut into 8 wedges each
malt vinegar and Classic Tartar Sauce (page 275) to serve

Pour oil to a depth of 3 inches in a deep skillet or deep-fryer. Heat oil to 375°F. In a bowl, whisk the beer batter ingredients together until smooth and the batter just coats the back of a spoon. Place the additional 1 cup flour on a plate. Dredge the fish in the flour and then in the batter, letting any excess batter drip off. Fry, in batches, until golden brown, about 4 minutes. Drain on paper towels, and salt to taste. Fry the potatoes, in batches, until golden brown, about 5 minutes. Drain on paper towels and salt to taste, and serve with the fish, along with malt vinegar and Tartar Sauce.

Serves 4

cornmeal-fried catfish

see variations page 121

Along the southern Mississippi River, farmers have carved out catfish ponds in the heavy, clay soil. Farm-raised catfish has a cleaner flavor than river-caught. It also tastes great in this classic dish from the American South, usually served with cornmeal fritters known as hush puppies.

vegetable oil for frying
1 cup yellow cornmeal
1 tsp. ground red pepper
1 tsp. fine kosher or sea salt
1/2 tsp. Hungarian paprika
1/2 tsp. ground black pepper

1/2 tsp. garlic powder
1/4 tsp. onion powder
1/4 tsp. ground dried thyme
1/4 tsp. dried oregano
2 lbs. farm-raised catfish fillets, rinsed and
    patted dry

Heat 1/2 inch of oil to 375°F in a large skillet. Combine the cornmeal and seasonings in a shallow bowl. Dredge the fish in the cornmeal mixture. When the oil is hot, fry the fish, turning once, until golden brown. Drain on paper towels and season to taste.

Serves 4

fritto misto with salsa verde

see variations page 122

Italian seafood fritto misto, usually served with the green sauce known as salsa verde, often features small whole fish known as whitebait or smelts, shrimp, calamari, and small sole. The batter is light and eggy, so serve with a fresh squeeze of lemon as well.

olive oil for frying
1 cup all-purpose flour
1 tsp. salt
1 tsp. ground white pepper
4 large eggs, beaten
8 oz. fresh whitebait or smelts, left whole
1 lb. raw large shrimp, peeled and deveined, tails on, rinsed, and patted dry

1 lb. small squid, heads removed, rinsed, and patted dry, body cut into rings, and tentacles
6 very small sole, cleaned and heads removed, rinsed, and patted dry
Salsa Verde (page 38) and lemon wedges, to serve

Heat 1/2 inch of olive oil to 375°F in a large skillet set over medium-high heat. Combine the flour and seasonings in a shallow bowl. Put the beaten eggs in a second bowl. Dredge the seafood in the flour mixture, then in the beaten eggs. When the oil is hot, fry the seafood, in batches, turning once, until golden brown. Drain on paper towels. Serve with the salsa and wedges of lemon.

Serves 6–8

sautéed sole with browned butter hollandaise

see variations page 123

Sweet, delicate fish meets deep, rich sauce in a taste marriage made in heaven. Smaller lemon sole, tilapia, turbot, or flounder fillets work best because they're flat and sauté quickly. For larger Dover sole or any fish fillet that won't fit in a sauté pan, broiling is the better option.

4 (6-oz.) lemon sole, tilapia, turbot,
    or flounder fillets
1 tbsp. butter
fine kosher or sea salt and ground black
    pepper to taste

fresh lemon wedges and minced Italian parsley,
    to garnish
Browned Butter Hollandaise (page 276),
    to serve

Rinse the fish under cold, running water and pat completely dry. Heat the butter in a heavy skillet over medium-high heat. When the butter starts to brown, add the fish and sauté for 4 or 5 minutes, turning once, or until the fish is opaque and lightly browned. Season to taste, garnish with lemon wedges and a sprinkle of Italian parsley, and serve with Browned Butter Hollandaise.

Serves 4

barbados-style fried fish

see variations page 124

In the waters off Barbados, flying fish zoom out of the water and dive back in—an amazing sight that people in Japan, Vietnam, Indonesia, and the Solomon Islands also see. In Barbados, however, flying fish have become a national symbol and a distinctively flavored dish.

1 small onion, quartered
1 tsp. dried thyme
1/4 cup chopped fresh Italian parsley
1 tsp. fresh lime juice
8 (6-oz.) flying fish, tilapia, farm-raised catfish, or sole fillets, rinsed and patted dry

fine kosher or sea salt and ground black pepper to taste
vegetable oil for frying
2 large eggs, beaten
2 cups fine dry breadcrumbs
lime wedges, to garnish

In a food processor, combine the onion, thyme, parsley, and lime juice. Process to a puree. Season the fish with salt and pepper to taste, then spread with the puree on the flesh side. Cover and refrigerate for 1 hour.

Heat 1/2 inch of oil to 375°F in a large skillet. When the oil is hot, carefully dip the fillets in the beaten eggs, then carefully roll in the breadcrumbs. Fry, in batches, turning once, until golden brown, about 6 minutes. Serve with lime wedges.

Serves 8

stir-fried red snapper with fragrant orange oil

see variations page 125

Stir-fried fish and vegetables get a final flourish of fragrant orange oil to finish. Serve with Coconut Rice (page 270), if you like.

for the fragrant orange oil
1/2 cup vegetable oil
1 tbsp. freshly grated orange zest
2 whole star anise
1 tbsp. black peppercorns

1 lb. red snapper fillet, rinsed and patted dry,
    and cut into 2-inch pieces
fine kosher or sea salt
1 tbsp. vegetable oil
3 green onions, sliced on the diagonal into
    2-inch pieces
1/2 lb. sliced mushrooms
1 cup thinly sliced Chinese or napa cabbage

To make the orange oil, heat the ingredients in a small saucepan over medium heat for 10 minutes. Remove from the heat and let steep for 30 minutes. Strain, then set aside. The orange oil will keep, covered in the refrigerator, for up to 2 weeks.

Season the fish with salt to taste. Heat the vegetable oil in a wok or large skillet over high heat until smoking. Add the green onions, mushrooms, and cabbage, and toss with paddles until the vegetables are wilted and browned. Add the fish and cook, stirring, until opaque. Serve each portion drizzled with 1 teaspoon of the orange oil.

Serves 4

variations

flash-fried calamari

see base recipe page 101

flash-fried clam strips
Prepare the basic recipe, using fresh clams cut into thin strips in place of calamari. Serve with Classic Tartar Sauce (page 275).

fried clam roll
Prepare the flash-fried clam strips variation above, serving the clam strips in a hot dog bun. Serve with Baja Slaw (page 266) and Classic Tartar Sauce (page 275).

aussie-style calamari
Instead of the basic recipe, marinate sliced calamari in a mixture of 2 beaten large eggs, 2 minced cloves garlic, 1 tablespoon soy sauce, and 1 teaspoon freshly grated gingerroot for 1 hour. Keep covered in the refrigerator. Heat 1/2 inch oil in a large skillet. Remove calamari from marinade and dust with 2 cups all-purpose flour. Fry in batches, turning once, until golden brown. Drain on paper towels and season to taste. Serve with sliced cucumber and prepared sweet chili sauce.

cajun calamari
Prepare the basic recipe, adding 1/4 cup Cajun or barbecue seasoning to the flour.

variations

whitefish beignets

see base recipe page 102

whitefish po' boy sandwich
Prepare the basic recipe. Split and toast 4 hoagie rolls or hot dog buns. Spread the inside of the rolls with Rémoulade (page 261). Top the bottom roll with shredded lettuce and thinly sliced tomatoes. Arrange the hot whitefish beignets on top of the tomatoes, replace the top bun, and serve.

oyster po' boy sandwich
Prepare the whitefish po'boy sandwich variation above, using shucked oysters in place of whitefish.

whitefish fingers
Prepare the basic recipe, cutting the whitefish into 6-inch-long pieces before dipping and frying.

lemony whitefish beignets
Prepare the basic recipe, using 1 teaspoon freshly grated lemon zest in place of the Cajun seasoning mixture.

shrimp beignets
Prepare the basic recipe, using 2 pounds shrimp in place of whitefish fillets.

variations

crab cakes

see base recipe page 105

whitefish cakes
Prepare the basic recipe, using 1 cup chopped whitefish or pollock fillets in place of crabmeat.

fresh salmon cakes
Prepare the basic recipe, using 1 cup chopped fresh salmon fillets in place of crabmeat. Serve with Rémoulade (page 261).

smoked salmon cakes
Prepare the basic recipe, using 1 cup chopped smoked salmon in place of crabmeat. Serve with Easy Aïoli (page 275).

lobster cakes
Prepare the basic recipe, using 1 cup chopped steamed lobster in place of crabmeat. Serve with Ancho-Lime Butter (page 257).

coconut prawns & jezebel sauce

see base recipe page 106

coconut oysters with jezebel sauce
Prepare the basic recipe, using 4 dozen shucked small oysters, in place of shrimp.

coconut prawn salad
Prepare the basic recipe. Arrange 8 cups baby greens on each of 8 plates. Divide 2 cups canned, drained, and chopped hearts of palm; 1 cup sectioned fresh orange; and 1 cup sliced green onion among the plates. Arrange 6 coconut prawns on each salad and drizzle with a double recipe of Asian Vinaigrette (page 27).

coconut prawns with sweet chili sauce
Prepare the basic recipe, using prepared sweet chili sauce for dipping. Garnish with cilantro and toasted peanuts.

variations

beer-battered fish 'n' chips

see base recipe page 108

beer-battered fish 'n' sweet potato fries
Prepare the basic recipe, using sweet potatoes in place of baking potatoes.

sake-battered fish 'n' taro chips
Prepare the basic recipe, using 1/2 cup sake and 1 1/2 cups water in place of beer and sliced taro root in place of potatoes.

sparkling wine-battered fish with hollandaise
Prepare the basic recipe, using 1 cup sparkling wine and 1 cup water in place of beer. Omit the potatoes. Serve with steamed spinach and Blender Hollandaise (page 264) instead of malt vinegar and Tartar Sauce.

beer-battered shrimp
Prepare the basic recipe, using raw large shrimp, peeled and deveined, in place of fish.

variations

cornmeal-fried catfish

see base recipe page 109

cornmeal-fried catfish nuggets
Prepare the basic recipe, using 2 pounds catfish nuggets or pieces in place of fillets.

cornmeal-fried catfish with fried green tomatoes
Prepare the basic recipe. Slice 2 large green tomatoes into 1/2-inch-thick slices. Dredge in the cornmeal mixture and fry, turning once, until golden brown.

cornmeal-fried lake perch
Prepare the basic recipe, using 2 pounds lake perch fillets in place of catfish. Serve with Classic Tartar Sauce (page 275).

southern fried tilapia
Prepare the basic recipe, using 1/2 cup yellow cornmeal and 1/2 cup all-purpose flour in place of all cornmeal. Use tilapia fillets in place of catfish.

variations

fritto misto with salsa verde

see base recipe page 110

shellfish fritto misto with salsa verde
Prepare the basic recipe, using 1 pound large shrimp, 1 pound shucked oysters, and 1 pound bay scallops in place of the variety of fish and shellfish.

seafood & vegetable fritto misto with salsa verde
Prepare the basic recipe, using 6 trimmed baby artichokes in place of the small sole and 1 pound trimmed asparagus in place of the whitebait. Fry the vegetables first, then the seafood.

fritto misto with aïoli
Prepare the basic recipe, serving it with Aïoli (page 262) in place of Salsa Verde.

catch-of-the-day fritto misto with salsa verde
Prepare the basic recipe, using 1 pound each of four different varieties of freshwater or ocean fish fillets cut into 4-inch pieces each in place of the variety of fish and shellfish.

sautéed sole with browned butter hollandaise

see base recipe page 112

sautéed sole with blood orange sauce

Prepare basic recipe, omitting hollandaise. Remove fish from skillet and swirl in 4 tablespoons butter until foaming. Whisk in the juice of a small blood orange. Season, pour over the fish, and serve.

sautéed sole with lemon–caper sauce

Prepare basic recipe, omitting hollandaise. Remove fish from skillet and swirl in 4 tablespoons butter until foaming. Whisk in 1–2 teaspoons fresh lemon juice and 1 tablespoon drained capers. Season, pour over the fish, and serve.

sautéed sole with mango chipotle sauce

Prepare basic recipe, omitting hollandaise. Remove fish from skillet. Add 2 cups chopped fresh mango to pan and sauté until softened, about 3 minutes. Add 1 tablespoon fresh lemon juice, 1 chopped canned chipotle in adobo sauce, and 1 teaspoon fresh lime juice. Serve on top of fish.

low-fat sole

Spray the inside of a skillet with cooking spray and heat over medium-high heat. When the skillet is hot, sauté the fish. Serve with a fresh salsa in place of hollandaise.

variations

barbados–style fried fish

see base recipe page 113

cartagena–style fried lobster

Instead of basic recipe, remove and chop meat from 4 medium lobster tails; reserve shells. Combine lobster with 2 tablespoons tomato paste, 1/4 cup chopped green onion, and 1 tablespoon Worcestershire sauce. Pack mixture into the shells. Carefully dip into 2 beaten eggs, then dredge in 2 cups fine dry breadcrumbs. Fry in vegetable oil, turning once, until browned on both sides.

tapas–style hake

Instead of basic recipe, process to smooth paste 1 small onion, 1/2 green bell pepper, 2 garlic cloves, and 2 tablespoons olive oil. Season 4 hake fillets with salt and pepper, then spread mixture on flesh side of fish. In skillet on medium-high heat, sauté fish, topping-side down, in 2 tablespoons olive oil for 4 minutes, then turn and sauté other side until fish is opaque, about 3 more minutes.

thai–style fried fish

Prepare basic recipe, spreading fish with 1 tablespoon green curry paste blended with 2 tablespoons coconut milk in place of the thyme mixture.

béarnaise–style fried fish

Prepare basic recipe, using 2 large shallots in place of onion, dried tarragon in place of thyme, and tarragon vinegar in place of lime juice.

stir-fried red snapper with fragrant orange oil

see base recipe page 114

stir-fried shrimp with fragrant orange oil
Prepare the basic recipe, using raw, large, peeled, and deveined shrimp in place of the fish. Cook shrimp until they are pink and opaque.

stir-fried red snapper with asian vinaigrette
Prepare the basic recipe, drizzling the cooked fish with Asian Vinaigrette (page 27) in place of orange oil.

stir-fried salmon & snow peas with fragrant orange oil
Prepare the basic recipe, using salmon in place of snapper and fresh snow peas in place of cabbage.

stir-fried scallops with fragrant orange oil
Prepare the basic recipe, using bay scallops in place of fish. Cook the scallops until they are opaque.

in the oven

Baked seafood dishes run the gourmet gamut from classic crab dip to buttered-and-breadcrumbed bay scallops served in a shell to traditional casseroles and trendy seafood flatbreads and pizzas.

classic crab dip

see variations page 142

With or without a disco ball and dancing, any great party needs one nibble that is sure to please everyone, and this is it. Serve it with savory crackers, small slices of dark rye bread, or toasted rounds of French bread.

8 oz. cream cheese, softened
1 tbsp. milk
6–7 oz. flaked, cooked crabmeat
3 tbsp. finely chopped onion
1/2–1 tsp. prepared horseradish

1/2 tsp. fine kosher or sea salt
1/2 tsp. ground black pepper
6 drops bottled hot pepper sauce
1 tsp. Worcestershire sauce

Preheat the oven to 375°F. Combine all ingredients in a bowl until well blended. Spoon the dip into a baking dish. Bake for 15 minutes or until bubbling. Serve hot.

Serves 8

baked scallops en coquille

see variations page 143

Large, clean scallop shells—available at better gourmet or kitchen stores—make perfect "plates" for this appetizer or first course.

1 garlic clove, minced
3 tbsp. fresh lemon juice
2 tbsp. finely chopped fresh Italian parsley
2 tbsp. olive oil

2 tbsp. butter, softened
8 large sea scallops, rinsed and patted dry
1/2 cup fine dry breadcrumbs

Preheat the oven to 425°F. Arrange 8 clean scallop shells or ovenproof ramekins on a cookie sheet. In a small bowl, combine the garlic, lemon juice, parsley, olive oil, and butter until well blended. Place a scallop in each shell or ramekin. Spoon the garlic mixture over each scallop and top each one with 1 tablespoon breadcrumbs. Bake for 10–15 minutes or until bubbling and golden. Serve hot with crusty bread.

Serves 8

lobster purses

see variations page 144

With a glass of bubbly, these rich lobster parcels make any occasion a celebration.

2 tbsp. sweet butter
3 tbsp. brandy
2 shallots, finely chopped
2 cloves garlic, minced
1 medium-sized carrot, finely chopped
1 cup dry white wine, preferably chardonnay

3 tbsp. heavy cream
kosher salt and freshly ground black pepper
   to taste
1 (17.5-oz.) package frozen puff pastry, thawed
meat from 2 large, cooked lobster tails, cut into
   6 (1/2-inch) pieces

In a large sauté pan, melt the butter. Add the brandy, light a long match, and carefully ignite. Let it burn for about 1 minute, being careful to stand back, then cover with a lid and let flames die out. Add the shallots, garlic, and carrot. Cook for 5 or 6 minutes, until tender. Add the white wine, bring to a boil, and reduce by half. Add the cream and turn off the heat. Season with salt and pepper.

Preheat the oven to 425°F. Cut the puff pastry sheets into 6 (6-inch) squares. Line a cookie sheet with parchment paper. Place 1 piece of lobster in the center of each square. Spoon about 2 teaspoons of the cream mixture atop lobster. Bring the corners of each puff pastry square together, moisten with water, and pinch closed to form a rectangular parcel. Place on the prepared cookie sheet. Bake the parcels for 20–25 minutes, until light golden brown and crispy. Serve warm.

Serves 6

thai shrimp flatbread

see variations page 145

With a cold beer and marinated cucumbers, this flatbread is delicious hot from the oven or at room temperature.

6 tbsp. creamy peanut butter
1/2 cup plain yogurt
2 tsp. brown sugar
1 1/2 tsp. soy sauce
1 tsp. toasted sesame oil
1 tsp. hot chili oil
2 tbsp. unseasoned rice wine vinegar

2 cloves garlic, minced
12 oz. cooked medium (31–35 count) shrimp, peeled and deveined
1 (12-inch) prebaked pizza crust
1/2 cup finely chopped red bell pepper
1/2 cup finely chopped green onions
1/2 cup chopped fresh cilantro, to garnish

Preheat the oven to 425°F. In a bowl, combine the peanut butter, yogurt, brown sugar, soy sauce, oils, rice vinegar, and garlic until smooth. Fold in the shrimp until well coated. Spread the mixture over the pizza crust so that the shrimp are in one layer. Top with bell pepper and green onions. Bake for 12–15 minutes or until the shrimp are opaque. Sprinkle with cilantro and serve.

Serves 4 as an entrée 8 as an appetizer

lobster quiche

see variations page 146

Rich and toothsome, this elegant quiche makes a fabulous brunch or lunch. Miniature quiches (see variation page 146) make bite-size appetizers.

1 (9-inch) deep-dish pie shell
1 cup chopped fresh baby spinach
6 oz. cooked lobster meat, chopped
1/4 cup diced red onion
1/4 cup diced red bell pepper

1 cup shredded Gruyère or Swiss cheese
4 large eggs
1 1/2 cups half-and-half or light cream
1/2 tsp. fine kosher or sea salt
1/2 tsp. freshly ground black pepper

Preheat the oven to 450°F. Prick the pie shell all over with the tines of a fork, and prebake for 5 minutes. Remove from oven and reduce the temperature to 350°F.

Arrange the spinach on the bottom of the crust. Top with the lobster, then the red onion and bell pepper. Scatter the cheese over the top. In a bowl, whisk together the eggs, half-and-half, salt, and pepper. Slowly pour the egg mixture over the lobster mixture in the pie shell. Bake for 35–45 minutes or until a knife inserted in the center comes out clean. Let cool for 15 minutes before slicing and serving.

Serves 6–8

baked halibut en papillote

see variations page 147

Baking seafood in parchment paper—along with aromatic herbs and flavorings—is a time-tested method that results in a moist, succulent dish, with little to no clean-up!

4 (16x16-inch) sheets parchment paper or
    heavy-duty aluminum foil
4 (6 oz.) halibut fillets (or pompano, grouper,
    bluefish, red snapper, cod, or catfish), rinsed
    and patted dry
2 cups sliced fresh mushrooms
2 cups canned Italian plum tomatoes, drained

1/4 cup chopped fresh tarragon
1/4 cup chopped fresh Italian parsley
1/4 cup dry white wine
1/4 cup extra-virgin olive oil
fine kosher or sea salt and freshly ground
    pepper to taste

Preheat the oven to 450°F. Lay each sheet of parchment paper on a flat surface and place a fish fillet in the middle of each. Top each fillet with 1/4 cup each of sliced mushrooms and tomatoes, and a tablespoon each of tarragon, parsley, white wine, and olive oil. Season. Fold the papers, crimping the edges closed, to form 4 packets and place on a cookie sheet. (The recipe can be prepared to this point, wrapped, and refrigerated for up to 1 day, if you wish.) Bake, seam-side up, for 14–16 minutes. Do not turn. To serve, place a packet on each plate, let cool slightly, then open.

Serves 4

brandade de morue with cherry tomatoes

see variations page 148

This traditional comfort food dish from the Mediterranean uses dried salt cod, usually available at Italian grocery stores. Allow 48 hours to soak the salt cod. Serve with French bread.

2 lbs. boneless salt cod
2 cups heavy cream
10 garlic cloves, peeled
1 lb. baking potatoes, peeled and diced
fine kosher or sea salt to taste

freshly ground white pepper to taste
1 pint cherry tomatoes
1/4 cup extra-virgin olive oil
2 tsp. chopped fresh thyme
2 tsp. chopped fresh rosemary

Soak the salt cod in cold water for 48 hours and change the water at least 4 times. Then, cut the salt cod into 8 pieces.

Preheat the oven to 400°F. In a saucepan, heat the cream, garlic, and salt cod pieces over medium-high heat until the fish is tender, about 8 minutes. Set aside. Place the potatoes in a large pot, cover with water, and bring to a boil. Cook until tender, about 15 minutes. Drain and mash the potatoes. Transfer the fish and cream mixture and mashed potatoes to a food processor and pulse to blend. Season. Spoon the mixture into the center of an oiled 8-inch square baking pan. Surround the brandade with the cherry tomatoes. Drizzle with olive oil, sprinkle with fresh herbs, and bake until bubbling, about 15 minutes.

Serves 6–8

banana leaf-wrapped barramundi

see variations page 149

Banana leaves, found fresh or frozen at Hispanic or Asian markets, lend a mild herbal flavor to fish while protecting the delicate flesh from the heat. Barramundi, native to Australian waters, are now farm-raised in the United States.

1 large banana leaf, fresh or frozen and thawed
    (or 1 large paper grocery sack)
1 whole baby barramundi (about 2–3 lbs.),
    cleaned and gutted, rinsed, and patted dry
olive oil for brushing

1 tsp. lemon pepper
1 tsp. fresh lime zest
kosher or sea salt and freshly ground black
    pepper to taste

Preheat the oven to 400°F. For a fresh banana leaf, remove center core and discard. Run the leaf under hot water until pliable. Pat leaf dry with paper towels and cut in half horizontally; overlap the two pieces so that they will cover the fish. For a frozen and thawed banana leaf, separate sections of the leaf and overlap two sections so that they will cover the fish.

Score the body of the fish with three slashes per side. Brush the fish with oil and season with lemon pepper, lime zest, salt, and pepper. Place fish on the banana leaves, fold in the left and right sides, and roll it up like a burrito. For a paper sack, insert the fish and fold the bag to close. Place the fish on a cookie sheet. Bake for 25 minutes or until the fish is firm and begins to flake when tested with a fork in the thickest part. To serve, carefully peel back the top wrapping and serve the fish on a platter.

Serves 4

shrimp & artichoke casserole

see variations page 150

A great dish for entertaining, this can be assembled ahead of time and doubled or tripled to serve a crowd. It has a flavor everyone loves.

1/2 lb. mushrooms, sliced
6 tbsp. butter
1 1/2 lbs. cooked medium (31–40 count) shrimp, peeled and deveined
10 canned artichoke hearts, drained and coarsely chopped
1/4 cup all-purpose flour

1 1/2 cups half-and-half or light cream
1/2 cup dry sherry
1 tbsp. Worcestershire sauce
fine kosher or sea salt and ground black pepper to taste
1/4 tsp. paprika
1/2 cup freshly grated Parmesan

Preheat the oven to 350°F. Sauté the mushrooms in 2 tablespoons of the butter until soft. Layer a 3-quart casserole dish with the mushrooms, shrimp, and artichoke hearts. In a saucepan, melt the remaining 4 tablespoons butter and whisk in the flour. Cook, whisking, for 3 minutes. Gradually pour in the half-and-half and whisk until the sauce has thickened. Add the sherry, Worcestershire sauce, salt, pepper, and paprika. Pour the sauce over the casserole ingredients and top with the Parmesan. Bake for 35–40 minutes or until browned and bubbling.

Serves 8

moroccan baked fish

see variations page 151

A spice caravan of flavor infuses this dish as it bakes. Serve it with a flatbread, such as pita or naan, warmed in the oven, or couscous to soak up all the juices.

1 large onion, thinly sliced
1 large tomato, thinly sliced
1 lemon, ends trimmed and thinly sliced
4 (6- to 8-oz.) fish fillets, such as red snapper,
   ocean perch, haddock, or John Dory, rinsed
   and patted dry
1 tbsp. ground cumin

1 tbsp. sweet Hungarian paprika
1 tbsp. ground coriander
1 tsp. ground caraway seeds
1/8 tsp. ground red pepper
fine kosher or sea salt
2 tbsp. olive oil

Preheat the oven to 375°F. Oil a 9x13-inch baking dish. Place a layer of onion, then tomato, then lemon in the baking dish. Place the fish fillets on the lemon slices. Combine the cumin, paprika, coriander, caraway, red pepper, and salt in a bowl. Sprinkle the spice mixture over the fish, then drizzle with olive oil. Cover and bake for 35 minutes or until the fish begins to flake when tested with a fork in the thickest part.

Serves 4

variations

classic crab dip

see base recipe page 127

classic shrimp dip
Prepare the basic recipe, using small canned shrimp, drained, in place of crab.

crab rangoon dip
Instead of the basic recipe, prepare Crab Rangoon (page 69), but bake it according to the Classic Crab Dip recipe. Serve Crab Rangoon Dip with fried wontons.

curried shrimp dip
Prepare the basic recipe, using small canned shrimp, drained, in place of crab. Use chopped green onions in place of onion and 1 teaspoon curry powder in place of horseradish and Worcestershire sauce.

crab-stuffed mushrooms
Prepare the basic recipe. Instead of spooning the crab dip into a baking dish, spoon it into 1 pound cleaned mushroom caps. Arrange the stuffed mushrooms on a cookie sheet and bake at 375°F until bubbling, about 15 minutes.

variations

baked scallops en coquille

see base recipe page 128

bay scallops en coquille
Prepare basic recipe, using 1 pound bay scallops in place of sea scallops and bake for just 8–10 minutes.

coquilles st. jacques
Instead of basic recipe, bring 1/4 cup dry white wine, 2 tablespoons fresh lemon juice, and 1 teaspoon dried tarragon to a boil. Whisk in 1 cup heavy cream and 2 teaspoons Dijon mustard. Cook, whisking, until mixture thickens. Divide 1 pound bay scallops among 8 ramekins. Spoon sauce over each and top with 1 tablespoon fine dry breadcrumbs. Bake at 425°F for 15 minutes or until bubbling.

archangels on horseback
Instead of the basic recipe, cut 4 slices of bacon in half lengthwise. Wrap 8 sea scallops in a half strip each and secure with toothpicks. Bake at 425°F for 12–15 minutes or until bacon has browned and scallops are opaque and firm.

angels on horseback
Prepare Archangels on Horseback variation above, using 8 large shucked oysters in place of sea scallops.

variations

lobster purses

see base recipe page 131

lobster purses with steamed spinach & browned butter hollandaise
Prepare basic recipe. Serve each lobster parcel on a bed of steamed spinach. Drizzle Browned Butter Hollandaise (page 276) around the perimeter of plate.

lobster purses with roasted asparagus & orange hollandaise
Prepare basic recipe. Serve each lobster parcel with roasted asparagus. Drizzle Orange Hollandaise (page 276) around the perimeter of plate.

lobster beggar's purses
Prepare lobster filling. In place of puff pastry, use 8 crepes. Spoon hot lobster filling into the center of each crepe and draw up sides to form a pouch. Secure the top with a blanched blade of fresh chive or a food-safe ribbon.

coquilles st. jacques purses
Prepare Coquille St. Jacques filling (page 143). In place of puff pastry, use 8 crepes. Spoon hot scallop filling into the center of each crepe and draw up the sides to form a pouch. Secure top with a blanched blade of fresh chive or a food-safe ribbon.

thai shrimp flatbread

see base recipe page 132

thai shrimp & chicken flatbread

Prepare basic recipe, using 6 ounces boneless, skinless chicken breast, cut into 2-inch pieces, in place of half the shrimp.

coconut green curry shrimp flatbread

Prepare basic recipe, using coconut milk in place of yogurt and 2 teaspoons green curry paste in place of soy sauce and sesame oil.

artichoke, shrimp & red bell pepper pizza

Instead of basic recipe, combine 12 ounces medium shrimp with 1/4 cup olive oil, 2 minced cloves garlic, salt, and pepper. Arrange 2 cups chopped canned artichoke hearts and 1 cup sliced red bell pepper on a pizza crust. Spoon the shrimp over and smooth so that they are in one layer. Scatter with 1/2 cup freshly grated Parmesan and bake at 425°F for 12–15 minutes.

white clam pizza

Prepare the Artichoke, Shrimp & Red Bell Pepper Pizza (above), but in place of shrimp, use 1 pound frozen and thawed chopped white clams.

variations

lobster quiche

see base recipe page 134

crab quiche
Prepare the basic recipe, using 6 ounces jumbo lump crabmeat in place
of lobster.

southern-style shrimp & bacon quiche
Prepare the basic recipe, using 1 cup cooked, peeled, deveined, and chopped
medium shrimp, and 1 cup cooked and crumbled bacon in place of lobster.
Use grated medium Cheddar in place of Gruyère.

crustless seafood quiche
Prepare the basic recipe, omitting the pie shell. Oil the inside of a 9-inch
baking dish. Arrange the lobster, vegetables, and cheese in the dish. Pour the
egg mixture over and bake according to the recipe.

miniature lobster quiches
Prepare the basic recipe, using 16–20 prepared, prebaked miniature tartlet
shells. Place a piece of lobster in each shell. Divide the vegetables and
cheese among the tartlets. Fill each shell with the egg mixture. Bake for
15–20 minutes or until browned and bubbling.

baked halibut en papillote

see base recipe page 135

foil-wrapped halibut on the grill
Prepare the basic recipe, using aluminum foil. Prepare a medium-hot fire in your grill. Place the foil packages on the grill, seam-side up, close the lid, and grill for 14–16 minutes.

sake sea bass on the grill
Instead of the basic recipe, use 4 (6-ounce) sea bass fillets in the center of a piece of aluminum foil. Top each with 2 tablespoons sake, 1 teaspoon soy sauce, 1/4 teaspoon freshly grated gingerroot, 1/4 teaspoon brown sugar, and 2 tablespoons chopped green onion. Prepare a medium-hot fire in your grill. Place the foil packages on the grill, seam-side up, close the lid, and grill for 14–16 minutes.

lemon-herb trout en papillote
Prepare the basic recipe, using trout in place of halibut. Omit tomatoes. Add 1 teaspoon fresh lemon juice to each trout before folding the parcels.

salmon en papillote
Prepare the basic recipe, using salmon in place of halibut.

variations

brandade de morue with cherry tomatoes

see base recipe page 136

brandade sandwich
Prepare basic recipe. Cut a French roll in half. Brush cut sides generously with olive oil. Place a lettuce leaf on the bottom, then top with 1/4 cup brandade, 1/4 cup baked cherry tomatoes, and the other half of the roll.

brandade-stuffed cherry tomatoes
Prepare basic brandade, drizzle with olive oil, and bake until bubbling. Scoop out a little of the flesh of each cherry tomato and cut a small slice off the bottom so it sits firmly. Stuff each tomato with 1 rounded teaspoon brandade, sprinkle with the herbs, and arrange on a platter.

brandade-stuffed mushrooms
Prepare basic brandade, omitting cherry tomatoes. Stuff 16 mushroom caps with the mixture, drizzle with olive oil, scatter with the herbs, and bake until bubbling.

brandade crostini
Prepare basic brandade, omitting tomatoes. Slice Italian or French bread, brush with olive oil, and toast at 350°F for 15 minutes. Spoon 1 tablespoon brandade on each slice. Drizzle with olive oil, sprinkle with herbs, and bake until warmed through.

banana leaf-wrapped barramundi

see base recipe page 138

grilled banana leaf-wrapped barramundi
Prepare the basic recipe. Prepare an indirect fire in your grill (the heat on one side, no heat on the other). Grill the leaf-wrapped barramundi over direct heat for 5 minutes on each side until the leaves are smoldering. Transfer the fish to the indirect side, close the grill lid, and grill for another 15 minutes.

grilled malaysian leaf-wrapped snapper
Prepare the basic recipe, using snapper in place of barramundi and slathering the fish with 1/2 cup prepared chili paste in place of the lemon pepper, lime zest, salt, and pepper. Grill as in the variation above.

rainforest leaf-wrapped fish
Prepare the basic recipe, using catfish, trout, or other freshwater fillets in place of whole barramundi. Season the fish before wrapping with 1/2 cup prepared achiote paste in place of the lemon pepper, lime zest, salt, and pepper.

barbadian leaf-wrapped fish
Prepare the basic recipe, using grouper in place of whole barramundi. Season the fish with fresh thyme in place of lemon pepper.

variations

shrimp & artichoke casserole

see base recipe page 139

crab & artichoke casserole
Prepare the basic recipe, using 8 ounces lump or flaked crabmeat in place of the shrimp.

shrimp mac & cheese
Prepare the basic recipe, omitting mushrooms, artichokes, sherry, and 2 tablespoons butter. Mix 2 cups cooked macaroni with the shrimp in the prepared casserole. Make the basic cream sauce, adding 1 cup grated aged sharp Cheddar cheese. Pour the sauce over the macaroni and shrimp, top with 1 additional cup grated Cheddar, and bake.

lobster mac & cheese
Prepare the Shrimp Mac & Cheese (above), using the cooked and chopped meat of 4 lobster tails in place of shrimp.

shrimp & artichoke pot pies
Prepare the basic recipe, using 8 oiled ovenproof ramekins instead of the 3-quart dish. Top each ramekin with a round of puff pastry. Bake at 425°F until the puff pastry is puffed and golden, about 15–20 minutes.

variations

moroccan baked fish

see base recipe page 140

lebanese baked fish

Prepare the basic recipe, using 1 tablespoon ground sumac, 1 tablespoon ground cumin, and 1 teaspoon salt in place of spice mixture. Mix 2 cloves minced garlic with the olive oil and drizzle over fish before baking.

italian baked fish

Prepare the basic recipe, using 1/4 cup dried Italian seasoning in place of seasoning mixture.

french fish gratin

Instead of the basic recipe, arrange 4 fish fillets, such as turbot, haddock, or halibut, in one layer in an oiled 9x13-inch baking dish. Pour 1/2 cup dry white wine and 1 tablespoon fresh lemon juice over fish. Cover and bake at 400°F for 20 minutes. Pour 1/2 cup heavy cream over the fish, sprinkle with 3/4 cup grated Gruyère, and bake, uncovered, until browned and bubbling, about 15 more minutes.

french scallop gratin

Prepare French Fish Gratin (above), using 1 pound bay scallops in place of fish.

on the grill

A hot fire, a slathering of olive oil, and a seasoning or marinade of your choice are all you need to grill perfect fish and shellfish. Grilling adds a caramelized flavor, plus you have a world of sauces and accompaniments that heighten the color and texture of each grilled dish.

grilled mini tuna "burgers" with rémoulade

see variations page 168

As a "little plates" tapas offering, these easy burgers go from grill to platter in minutes. Tuna is one fish that tastes best when seared and served rare or when grilled to medium.

1/4 cup olive oil, plus extra for brushing
2 tbsp. tarragon vinegar
1 bay leaf, crumbled
8 small artisanal rolls such as ciabattini, sliced in half

8 (3-oz.) yellowfin tuna steaks, cut 1-inch thick, rinsed, and patted dry
Rémoulade (page 261), to serve

Prepare a hot fire in your grill. In a small bowl, mix together the olive oil, tarragon vinegar, and bay leaf. Brush the cut sides of the rolls with more olive oil. Grill the tuna steaks for 2 1/2–3 minutes per side for medium-rare (3–4 minutes for medium). Baste with the oil and tarragon mixture several times while grilling. Only turn fish once. During the last few minutes of grilling, place the rolls, cut-sides down, on the grill rack, and grill until the bread is golden and has good grill marks. To serve, place a tuna steak in each roll and top with the Rémoulade.

Serves 8

rum & lime-grilled shrimp on the barbie

see variations page 169

Australian slang for a barbecue grill, the "barbie" lends a caramelized, slightly smoky flavor to shrimp sizzled on it. Shellfish continue to cook for a minute or two after you grill them, so pull them off the grill right before you think they're done. To make sure the shrimp get evenly grilled, thread them on the skewers without crowding.

6 (12-inch) bamboo skewers
1/4 cup (4 tbsp.) sweet butter, melted
2 tbsp. freshly squeezed lime juice (from about 2 limes)
2 tbsp. dry sherry or rum (white or dark)

2 finely chopped green onions with some of the green
2 tsp. freshly grated gingerroot
24 raw, large (21–30 count) shrimp, peeled and deveined, rinsed, and patted dry

Soak the bamboo skewers in water for 30 minutes. Prepare a hot fire in your grill. In a bowl, whisk together the melted butter, lime juice, sherry or rum, green onions, and gingerroot. Thread the shrimp onto the skewers. Reserve one-fourth of the lime mixture; brush the shrimp liberally with the rest. Grill the skewers for 2–4 minutes per side or until the shrimp are firm, opaque, and have good grill marks. Serve the skewers drizzled with the reserved baste.

Serves 6 as an entrée, 12 as an appetizer

beachside grilled mackerel

see variations page 170

For the best flavor, grill and eat oily fish like mackerel, herring, anchovies, and sardines as soon after they're caught as possible. A driftwood fire on the beach and a tangy finishing sauce of Dijon mustard, butter, and lemon make the most of these delicious fish.

4 (1-lb.) mackerel, dressed, rinsed, and
    patted dry
4 tbsp. sweet butter, melted
1 tsp. Dijon mustard
1 tsp. fresh lemon juice

1/4 cup finely chopped fresh Italian parsley
fine kosher or sea salt and freshly ground
    pepper to taste
lemon wedges, to garnish

Make 2 or 3 slashes on each side of the fish. Press each mackerel open, like a book. Combine the melted butter, mustard, lemon juice, and parsley. Brush the fish, inside and out, with the melted butter mixture, then season to taste.

Prepare a hot fire in your grill. Oil a perforated grill rack and place the mackerel, still open like a book, skin-side down, on the grill rack. Grill the fish for 10 minutes or until the flesh flakes easily when tested with a fork in the thickest part. Do not turn. (Mackerel are so thin you don't have to turn them.) Serve garnished with lemon wedges.

Serves 4

campfire trout

see variations page 171

It may not be instant gratification, but close to it when you can grill fish you've just caught. Here's an easy way to do it. You can also use fresh-caught lake perch, bluegill, crappie, or walleye pike.

4 (12-oz.) whole trout, cleaned, rinsed, and patted dry
4 tbsp. olive oil, plus more for brushing
16 lemon slices, cut 1/8-inch thick

8 branches fresh rosemary
fine kosher or sea salt and freshly ground black pepper to taste

Prepare a campfire outdoors or a wood fire in a charcoal grill or a fireplace, using seasoned hardwoods such as oak, maple, or hickory. (Do not use pine, as it lends a resin-like taste and causes flare-ups.) Place each trout, skin-side down, on a flat surface. Drizzle 1 tablespoon olive oil in the cavity of each fish, then place 4 lemon slices and 2 branches of rosemary in the cavity. Brush each trout with more olive oil and season to taste. Place the fish in two oiled, hinged grill baskets. When the coals have turned gray and you have a medium-hot fire, grill the fish in the baskets for 5 minutes on one side, then turn baskets over and cook the fish on the other side. Keep turning until the fish begins to flake easily when tested with a fork in the thickest part, but is still moist, about 15 minutes total.

Serves 4

grilled yabbies with ginger-lime sauce

see variations page 172

Yabbies are Australian freshwater crustaceans, much like crayfish or lobster. Like lobster, you boil or steam them first, then add the flavor of the grill. In North America, use jumbo shrimp, spot shrimp, langoustines, or large crayfish.

4 tbsp. olive oil, divided, plus more for brushing
juice of 1 lime
1/4 cup chopped fresh cilantro leaves
2 tsp. freshly grated gingerroot

kosher or sea salt to taste
2 lbs. jumbo shrimp, spot shrimp, langoustines,
    or large crayfish, uncooked, shells on,
    deveined, rinsed, and patted dry

Prepare a medium-hot fire in your grill. In a bowl, whisk the olive oil, lime juice, cilantro, and gingerroot together. Season to taste. Bring a large pot of salted water to a boil. Add the shrimp and cook until they turn red, about 5 or 6 minutes. Immediately remove the shrimp with tongs, run under cold water, and transfer to a cutting board. With a large, sharp knife, remove the tail shells only and discard. Brush shrimp on all sides with olive oil. Place the shrimp on the grill, cover, and grill for 2 minutes. Turn the shrimp, cover, and grill again for 2 minutes. Serve drizzled with Ginger-Lime Sauce (page 39).

Serves 6

woo hoo grilled halibut with papaya salsa

see variations page 173

Woo hoo is right! First you get the hit of hot piri-piri sauce, then the sweetness of the fish, then the cooling salsa. Only marinate the fish for a short time—under 30 minutes— or the tender fish could be "cooked" by the acid in the marinade and you'll have ceviche instead. Piri-piri is made from hot peppers brought to southern Africa by Portuguese explorers by way of South America.

4 (6-oz.) halibut fillets (or pompano, grouper, bluefish, red snapper, cod, or catfish), rinsed and patted dry
1–2 tsp. bottled piri-piri or other hot pepper sauce
2 cloves garlic, minced

2 tsp. fresh lemon juice
1/4 cup canola oil
fine kosher or sea salt and freshly ground black pepper to taste
Papaya & Lime Salsa (page 277), to serve

Prepare a hot fire in your grill. In a bowl, combine the piri-piri sauce, garlic, lemon juice, and canola oil. Season to taste. Brush the marinade over both sides of the fish and let marinate for just 30 minutes.

Measure how thick the fish is in the thickest part (it's usually about 3/4 inch). Calculate your grilling time based on 10 minutes per inch of thickness (about 7 1/2 minutes total for a 3/4-inch-thick fillet). So grill the fish for 3 1/2–4 minutes per side, turning once, or until the fish begins to flake when tested with a fork in the thickest part. Serve with the salsa.

Serves 4

baja fish tacos

see variations page 174

Famous in Baja California, these fish tacos have a delicate texture yet a hearty grill flavor. Enjoy them with a pitcher of Mexican beer or a frosty margarita.

1/2 head red cabbage, cored and thinly sliced
2 tbsp. white vinegar
salt and ground black pepper to taste
2 ripe avocados, peeled and pitted
1/2 cup sour cream
2 tbsp. fresh lime juice

6 skinless mahi mahi, pompano, yellow snapper, halibut, or cod fillets, rinsed and patted dry
vegetable oil
warm flour tortillas, to serve
chopped fresh cilantro, to garnish

Combine the red cabbage and vinegar in a medium bowl and season to taste. Puree the avocados, sour cream, and lime juice in a food processor or blender; season to taste.

Prepare a hot fire in your grill. Brush the fish with oil, then season to taste. Measure how thick the fish is in the thickest part (it's usually about 3/4 inch). Grill the fish, turning once, for 10 minutes per inch of thickness (about 7 1/2 minutes for a 3/4-inch-thick fillet).

To serve, cut the fish into strips and place in warm tortillas. Garnish with the slaw, avocado cream, and cilantro.

Serves 6

seared scallops with roasted red bell pepper & basil puree

see variations page 175

Sweet, meaty sea scallops continue to cook for at least a minute after you take them off the grill, so once they have a good, seared crust, they're basically done. So don't overcook!

1 (12-oz.) jar roasted red bell peppers, drained
4 tbsp. sweet butter, softened
fine kosher or sea salt and freshly ground black
    pepper to taste

20 medium sea scallops (about 1 lb.), rinsed
    and patted dry
olive oil for brushing
1/4 cup fresh basil leaves, stacked together, and
    cut into chiffonade strips

Prepare a hot fire in your grill. Place a cast-iron grill griddle or skillet on the grill grate and let it get hot enough that a drop of water sizzles immediately. Place the roasted red bell peppers and butter in a food processor and process until pureed. Season to taste. Brush the scallops with olive oil and season to taste. Grill scallops on the hot griddle or in the hot skillet for 2 minutes per side or until the scallops are seared and almost opaque. Stir the basil chiffonade into the roasted red pepper puree. Serve the scallops atop the puree.

Serves 4

stir-grilled salmon with cherry tomatoes & sugar snap peas

see variations page 176

Stir-grilling involves marinating foods cut into small pieces, then placing them in a perforated metal grill wok over a hot fire. You use wooden paddles or grill spatulas to stir-grill the food, giving it a great grill flavor as it cooks. Serve with steamed rice, if you like.

Asian Vinaigrette (page 27) or bottled
   teriyaki sauce
1 lb. skinless salmon fillet, rinsed and patted
   dry, cut into 2-inch pieces

12 cherry tomatoes
1/2 lb. fresh sugar snap peas
1/2 red onion, cut into small wedges

Place the vinaigrette in a sealable plastic bag. Add the salmon, tomatoes, peas, and onion. Seal, toss to blend, and refrigerate for 30 minutes. Prepare a hot fire in your grill. Set an oiled grill wok on the grill rack. Transfer the salmon mixture to the grill wok using a slotted spoon. Stir-grill the salmon and vegetables for 8 minutes, using long-handled wooden paddles or grill spatulas to toss.

Close the lid of the grill to heat through for another 5 minutes before serving.

Serves 4

grilled swordfish with tomato-spinach orzo

see variations page 177

Swordfish is one of the few fish that you can still get cut into steaks. It's a meaty, oily fish from the colder, deeper waters of the Atlantic and Mediterranean. Rosemary and garlic really accentuate its flavor and firmer texture.

1/4 cup olive oil
1 tsp. dried rosemary
1 clove garlic, minced
fine kosher or sea salt and freshly ground black
    pepper to taste

4 swordfish steaks, cut 1-inch thick, rinsed, and
    patted dry
Tomato-Spinach Orzo (page 268), to serve

Combine the olive oil, rosemary, garlic, and seasonings in a bowl. Brush all over the swordfish and let rest for 30 minutes. Prepare a hot fire in your grill. Grill the swordfish for 4–5 minutes per side, turning once, or until you have good grill marks and the swordfish is firm to the touch. Serve with the orzo.

Serves 4

grilled mini tuna "burgers" with rémoulade

see base recipe page 153

mini salmon "burgers" with rémoulade
Prepare basic recipe, using salmon steaks or small fillets in place of tuna.

tuna burgers with hoisin & pickled ginger
Instead of basic recipe, finely mince 2 pounds fresh tuna (skin and bones removed) with a sharp knife or pulse in a food processor. Season with 1 1/2 teaspoons salt and 1 teaspoon black pepper. Form 8 patties. Grill for 2 1/2–3 minutes per side. Serve on buns with hoisin sauce and pickled ginger.

indoor-grilled mini tuna "burgers" with rémoulade
Prepare basic recipe, but grill burgers on stove in a heavy grill pan preheated over high heat for 15 minutes (or until very, very hot).

open-face swordfish burgers with tarragon hollandaise
Prepare basic recipe, using swordfish steaks instead of tuna and Tarragon Hollandaise (page 276) in place of rémoulade. Combine 1/2 cup chopped fresh tomato, 1/2 cup chopped pitted Kalamata olives, and 2 tablespoons capers. Top each burger with hollandaise, then with some tomato mixture. Serve open-faced on grilled country bread.

variations

rum & lime-grilled shrimp on the barbie

see base recipe page 154

rum & lime-grilled scallops on the barbie
Prepare the basic recipe, using 24 medium sea scallops in place of shrimp.

chili-basted indonesian shrimp
Instead of the basic recipe, baste the shrimp with 1/2 cup prepared chili-garlic paste before grilling. Serve with Mango & Lime Salsa (page 265).

shrimp teppanyaki
Instead of the basic recipe, brush the shrimp with canola oil before putting them on the grill. As they grill, baste them with 1/2 cup prepared teriyaki sauce. Serve with grilled rings of fresh pineapple and fried rice.

balinese shrimp satay
Instead of the basic recipe, make Satay Sauce by mixing 2 teaspoons Thai red curry paste, 1 1/2 cups coconut milk, 1/2 cup chunky peanut butter, and 1 teaspoon tamarind paste or freshly squeezed lime juice until smooth. Stir in 1/4 cup finely chopped fresh cilantro leaves. Brush the shrimp with some of the Satay Sauce before putting them on the grill. Serve with sliced cucumber, the remaining Satay Sauce, and Coconut Rice (page 270).

variations

beachside grilled mackerel

see base recipe page 157

beachside grilled bluefish
Prepare the basic recipe, using small bluefish or bluefish fillets in place
of mackerel.

grilled sardines marseilles-style
Instead of the basic recipe, use 1 pound dressed, fresh sardines in place of
mackerel. Brush the fish all over with olive oil and sprinkle with dried fennel,
salt, and pepper. Grill according to the recipe, then serve garnished with
lemon wedges.

barbadian pompano
Instead of the basic recipe, use small pompano or pompano fillets in place of
mackerel. Brush the fish all over with olive oil and drizzle with 2 tablespoons
fresh lime juice. Sprinkle with 1 teaspoon dried thyme and salt and pepper to
taste. Grill according to the recipe, then serve garnished with lime wedges.

asian-style amberjack
Instead of the basic recipe, use amberjack fillets in place of mackerel. Brush the
fish all over with prepared teriyaki sauce. Grill according to the recipe, then
serve with steamed rice and Asian Vinaigrette (page 27).

campfire trout

see base recipe page 158

skillet-grilled trout
Prepare basic recipe, using 2 seasoned cast-iron skillets in place of grill baskets. Drizzle an extra tablespoon of olive oil over exterior of each trout. Place skillets on a grate over campfire, grill, or in fireplace and heat until very hot. Add fish and grill, turning once, about 15 minutes total.

grilled bacon-wrapped trout
Instead of basic recipe, put 2 tablespoons chopped green onions inside each fish, season with salt and pepper, wrap in 3 bacon slices, secure with toothpicks, and grill.

grilled leaf-wrapped trout
Prepare basic recipe, adding 16 grape, cabbage, or romaine lettuce leaves blanched in boiling water for 1 minute or until just wilted, then drained and patted dry. Wrap each fish in 4 leaves and secure with toothpicks before grilling.

pancetta-wrapped perch
Instead of basic recipe, season 4 lake perch inside and out with salt and pepper. Place 3 basil leaves inside each fish, then wrap each fish in 1 or 2 slices pancetta and secure with toothpicks. After grilling, serve with Aïoli (page 262).

variations

grilled yabbies with ginger-lime sauce

see base recipe page 160

grilled yabbies with asian vinaigrette
Prepare the basic recipe, using Asian Vinaigrette (page 27) in place of
Ginger-Lime Sauce.

grilled spot shrimp with herbed tomato vinaigrette
Prepare the basic recipe, using spot shrimp in place of yabbies and Herbed
Tomato Vinaigrette (page 258) in place of Ginger-Lime Sauce.

grilled yabbie salad
Prepare the basic recipe. Arrange the grilled yabbies over salad greens and
drizzle with the sauce.

grilled yabbie-stuffed tomato
Prepare the basic recipe, omitting the sauce. Combine 1 1/2 cups grilled
yabbies with 1 tablespoon Dijon mustard, 1/2 cup mayonnaise, 1 tablespoon
fresh dill weed, and salt and white pepper to taste. Core and hollow out
6 large ripe tomatoes and stuff with the yabbie mixture. Serve chilled.

woo hoo grilled halibut with papaya salsa

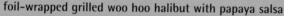

see base recipe page 161

foil-wrapped grilled woo hoo halibut with papaya salsa
Prepare the basic recipe, wrapping each marinated fillet in aluminum foil.
Prepare a medium-hot fire in your grill. Place the foil packages on the grill,
seam-side up, close the lid, and grill for 14–16 minutes.

woo hoo halibut in parchment parcels with papaya salsa
Prepare the basic recipe, but instead of grilling, preheat the oven to 450°F.
Place a marinated fillet in the center of a 16-inch parchment paper square.
Fold into a parcel and bake for 14–16 minutes.

woo hoo halibut skewers with papaya salsa
Prepare the basic recipe. Soak 12 bamboo skewers in water for 30
minutes. Cut the marinated fish into 3-inch pieces and thread onto the
skewers, taking care not to crowd the fish. Grill for 4 minutes on each
side, turning once.

thai-style grilled halibut with papaya salsa
Prepare the basic recipe, using 1 tablespoon green curry paste mixed with
1/4 cup coconut milk in place of the marinade.

variations

baja fish tacos

see base recipe page 162

baja shrimp tacos
Prepare the basic recipe, using grilled shrimp in place of fish.

baja seared tuna tacos
Prepare the basic recipe, using slices of grill-seared tuna in place of fish.

baja swordfish tacos
Prepare the basic recipe, using grilled swordfish steaks seasoned with smoked paprika in place of fish.

baja lobster tacos
Prepare the basic recipe, using steamed lobster tail meat, cut into pieces, in place of fish.

variations

seared scallops with roasted red bell pepper & basil puree

see base recipe page 164

seared scallops with sweet pea puree
Prepare the basic recipe. In place of the roasted red bell pepper and basil puree, cook 1 (10-ounce) package frozen petit pois in boiling salted water for 3 minutes or until just tender. Drain, then puree in the food processor with 4 tablespoons butter and salt and pepper to taste.

seared scallops with butternut squash & parmesan puree
Prepare the basic recipe. In place of the roasted red bell pepper and basil puree, heat 1 (15-oz.) can butternut squash puree with 1/4 cup freshly grated Parmesan in a saucepan until warmed through and the cheese has melted. Season to taste.

prosciutto-wrapped scallops
Prepare the basic recipe, wrapping each scallop with a strip of prosciutto and securing with a toothpick before grilling.

seared monkfish with roasted red bell pepper & basil puree
Prepare the basic recipe, using 4 monkfish fillets in place of scallops, grilled for 10 minutes per inch of thickness, turning once.

variations

stir-grilled salmon with cherry tomatoes & sugar snap peas

see base recipe page 165

stir-grilled shrimp with cherry tomatoes & sugar snap peas
Prepare basic recipe, using raw, large, peeled, and deveined shrimp in place of salmon.

stir-grilled catfish with corn, cherry tomatoes & zucchini
Prepare basic recipe, using 1 cup bottled Italian dressing in place of Asian Vinaigrette, farm-raised catfish fillets in place of salmon, and 1 cup uncooked fresh corn and 1 cup thinly sliced zucchini in place of peas.

stir-grilled shrimp satay
Prepare basic recipe, using Satay Sauce (page 169) in place of Asian Vinaigrette, raw peeled and deveined shrimp (or jumbo shrimp) in place of salmon, and 1 cup sliced red bell pepper and 1 cup chopped scallions in place of peas and red onion. Garnish with roasted peanuts.

stir-grilled pacific rim mahi mahi
Prepare basic recipe, using bottled teriyaki sauce in place of Asian Vinaigrette, mahi mahi in place of salmon, 1 cup sliced red bell pepper and 1 cup chopped fresh pineapple in place of peas, and 1/2 cup chopped scallions in place of red onion.

grilled swordfish with tomato-spinach orzo

see base recipe page 166

grilled swordfish with cucumber-dill orzo
Prepare basic recipe, using Cucumber-Dill Orzo (page 279) in place of
Tomato-Spinach Orzo.

rosemary-infused grilled swordfish with tomato-spinach orzo
Prepare basic recipe, omitting the dried rosemary. Add 2 branches of fresh
rosemary to the olive oil, garlic, and seasonings in microwave-safe bowl and
cook on high heat for 1 minute. Let steep and cool for 15 minutes. Pour the
infused oil over the swordfish steaks and let them infuse at room
temperature for 30 minutes before grilling.

grilled swordfish with fresh herb butter & tomato-spinach orzo
Prepare basic recipe, topping each grilled swordfish steak with a pat of Fresh
Herb Butter (page 272) before serving.

marinated grilled swordfish with tomato-spinach orzo
Instead of the rosemary vinaigrette, whisk together 2 tablespoons fresh
lemon juice, 2 minced cloves garlic, 1 teaspoon sea salt, and 1/4 cup olive oil
to make a marinade. Pour the marinade over the swordfish steaks and
marinate at room temperature for 30 minutes. Remove steaks from
marinade and grill as in basic recipe.

on a plank

With planked seafood, you get the gentle, aromatic flavor of the wood quite deliciously different from the flavor of grilling or smoking. Planking is the simplest way to cook on the grill—just place the plank on the grill and close the lid. Yum!

planked shrimp with bistro butter

see variations page 194

In this recipe, the shrimp (or jumbo shrimp) take on the aromatic wood flavor of the plank while being basted with the Bistro Butter while they cook. You can serve this right from the plank with plenty of crusty bread to mop up the juices.

1 oven plank, soaked in water for at least
   30 minutes
16–24 large raw shrimp (or jumbo shrimp),
   peeled and deveined, rinsed, and patted dry
Bistro Butter (page 272)

While the plank soaks, prepare an indirect fire in your grill (with heat on one side, no heat on the other). Arrange the shrimp in one layer on the soaked plank, with as much of the shrimp touching the wood as possible (for more aromatic wood flavor). Dot the butter over the shrimp. Place the plank on the indirect (no heat) side of the grill, close the lid, and cook for 30–45 minutes, or until the shrimp are pink and opaque. Serve right away.

Serves 4

planked salmon chimichurri

see variations page 195

When you plank a salmon fillet, you don't have to worry about turning it on the grill—it's cooked on the plank. Easy! Chimichurri Sauce is a fresh herb vinaigrette from Argentina that really complements salmon. This dish is delicious as an entrée—serve it right from the plank if you like—or as an appetizer with grilled bread, slathered with more Chimichurri.

1 oven plank, soaked in water for at least
    30 minutes
1 skinless salmon fillet, rinsed and patted dry,
    and cut to fit the plank

Chimichurri (page 273)
grilled bread, to serve

While the plank soaks, prepare an indirect fire in your grill (heat on one side, no heat on the other). Place the salmon on the plank. Drizzle the fish with Chimichurri. Place on the indirect (no heat) side of the grill, close the lid, and cook for 45–60 minutes, or until the salmon begins to flake when tested with a fork in the thickest part. Serve right away.

Serves 6 as an entrée, 12 as an appetizer

macadamia-buttered barramundi

see variations page 196

Get a taste of Australia and New Zealand with this dish. Barramundi are now farm-raised in North America, or you can substitute Tasmanian ocean trout, Arctic char, hake, haddock, or monkfish—all medium-textured fish with great flavor.

for the macadamia butter
1/2 cup finely chopped macadamia nuts
1 stick (4 oz.) sweet butter, softened
1/4 cup finely chopped fresh Italian parsley
fine kosher or sea salt and freshly ground black
    pepper to taste

1 oven plank, soaked in water for at least
    30 minutes
2 lbs. skinless barramundi fillets, rinsed and
    patted dry
lime wedges, to garnish

For the Macadamia Butter, combine the nuts, butter, and parsley in a bowl and stir together with a fork. Season to taste.

While the plank soaks, prepare an indirect fire in your grill (heat on one side, no heat on the other). Place the barramundi on the soaked plank. Dollop the Macadamia Butter over the fish. Place on the indirect (no heat) side of the grill, close the lid, and cook for 45–60 minutes, or until the barramundi begins to flake when tested with a fork in the thickest part. Garnish with lime wedges.

Serves 6

alder-planked tilapia with artichoke glaze

see variations page 197

Alder, a hardwood from the Pacific Northwest, adds a gentle woodsy flavor to the fish. The artichoke glaze, a built-in sauce, adds even more flavor while keeping the fish moist and delicious.

for the artichoke glaze
1/2 cup chopped canned artichoke hearts, drained
1 cup mayonnaise
1/2 cup freshly grated Asiago cheese

freshly ground white pepper to taste
2 alder planks, soaked in water for at least 30 minutes
4 skinless tilapia fillets, rinsed and patted dry
lime wedges, to garnish

Prepare an indirect fire in your grill (heat on one side, no heat on the other). For the Artichoke Glaze, combine the artichokes, mayonnaise, and Asiago in a bowl. Stir together with a fork, then season to taste. Place the tilapia on the soaked planks. Spread the glaze over the fish. Place on the indirect (no heat) side of the grill, close the lid, and cook for 30 minutes, or until the tilapia begins to flake when tested with a fork in the thickest part. Garnish with lime wedges.

Serves 4

planked monkfish tapas

see variations page 198

For a wonderful warm weather party, serve this colorful fish appetizer with grilled bread and a dollop or two of Aïoli (page 262), along with a chilled sangria.

for the topping
1/2 cup olive oil
2 cloves garlic, minced
1/2 cup chopped red bell pepper
1/2 cup chopped green onion
1 tsp. sherry vinegar or fresh lemon juice, or
    to taste

fine kosher or sea salt and freshly ground black
    pepper to taste
2 cedar, oak, or maple planks, soaked in water
    for at least 30 minutes
4 skinless monkfish fillets, rinsed and
    patted dry

Prepare an indirect fire in your grill (heat on one side, no heat on the other). For the topping, combine the olive oil, garlic, bell pepper, green onion, and sherry vinegar in a food processor. Pulse until very finely chopped. Season to taste.

Place the monkfish on the soaked planks. Spread the topping over the fish. Place on the indirect (no heat) side of the grill, close the lid, and cook for 45–60 minutes, or until the monkfish begins to flake when tested with a fork in the thickest part. Serve immediately.

Serves 8 as an appetizer

tuna niçoise on a plank

see variations page 199

In this new take on the classic recipe from Nice, all the star ingredients go on the plank, then they are served over fresh greens. Enjoy with a glass of chilled rosé and a crusty baguette.

1/4 cup red wine vinegar
2 tbsp. minced shallot
1 tbsp. Dijon mustard
1 large clove garlic, minced
1 tsp. anchovy paste
3/4 cup extra-virgin olive oil
fine kosher or sea salt and freshly ground black
    pepper to taste
1 oven plank or 2 thin planks, soaked in water
    for at least 30 minutes

4 fresh tuna steaks, cut 1-inch thick, rinsed,
    and patted dry
3/4 lb. thin string beans or haricots verts, fresh
    or frozen, trimmed
2 cups cherry or grape tomatoes
3 large hard-boiled eggs, shelled and quartered
1 cup brine- or oil-cured niçoise olives
4 cups fresh leafy greens, to serve
1 1/2 tbsp. finely chopped fresh basil,
    to garnish

Prepare an indirect fire in your grill (heat on one side, no heat on the other). For the Red Wine Vinaigrette, combine the red wine vinegar, shallot, Dijon mustard, garlic, anchovy paste, and olive oil in a bowl, and whisk to blend. Season to taste. Place the tuna on the soaked plank(s). Arrange the beans, cherry tomatoes, eggs, and olives over the tuna. Drizzle with half of the vinaigrette. Place on the indirect (no heat) side of the grill, close the lid, and cook for 30 minutes, or until the beans are crisp-tender. Arrange the salad greens on 4 plates and top with the tuna, beans, cherry tomatoes, eggs, and olives. Drizzle with the remaining vinaigrette and top with the basil.

Serves 4

planked mahi mahi with fresh pineapple salsa

see variations page 200

Fresh salsas are also delicious as built-in sauces for planked seafood. Just remember to brush the fish or shellfish with olive oil first to help keep them moist and protected from the heat of the grill.

2 thin planks, soaked in water for at least
   30 minutes
6 skinless mahi mahi fillets (or pompano, yellow
   snapper, halibut, or cod), rinsed and
   patted dry
olive oil for brushing

salt and ground black pepper to taste
Pineapple & Lime Salsa (page 277)
warm flour tortillas, to serve
sour cream and chopped fresh cilantro,
   to garnish

Prepare an indirect fire in your grill (heat on one side, no heat on the other). Brush the mahi mahi with olive oil and season to taste. Place the mahi mahi on the plank(s) and top with the salsa. Place on the indirect (no heat) side of the grill, close the lid, and cook for 30–45 minutes, or until the fish begins to flake when tested with a fork in the thickest part.

To serve, cut the salsa-topped fish into chunks and place in warm flour tortillas, garnished with sour cream and cilantro.

Serves 6

smoke-planked lemon–tarragon snapper

see variations page 201

By adding wood chips to the fire, you can add a kiss of smoke to seafood that you plank. Serve this as a main course with Lemon Rice (page 281) or as an appetizer with gourmet crackers.

2 thin planks, soaked in water at least
    30 minutes
1 cup dry hardwood chips or pellets, such as
    mesquite, hickory, or pecan
4 tbsp. sweet butter, softened

1/4 cup snipped fresh tarragon leaves
1 tbsp. fresh lemon juice
4 red snapper fillets, rinsed and patted dry
fine kosher or sea salt and freshly ground black
    pepper to taste

Soak the planks while you prepare an indirect fire in your grill (heat on one side, no heat on the other). For a gas grill, place 1 cup dry wood chips in an aluminum foil packet, seal, then poke holes in the top for the smoke to escape. Place packet near a burner. For a charcoal grill, scatter the wood chips on hot coals.

In a bowl, combine the butter, tarragon, and lemon juice. Place the snapper on the planks, spread the Lemon-Tarragon Butter over the snapper, and season to taste. Place the planks on the indirect (no heat) side of the grill. When you see the first wisp of smoke, close the lid, and cook for 30–45 minutes, or until the fish begins to flake when tested with a fork in the thickest part.

Serves 4 as an entrée, 8 as an appetizer

cedar-planked sole roulade

see variations page 202

Use a very thin fish for this fancier dish, such as sole, flounder, or turbot. Spread the fillet with the filling, then roll up, place on the plank, and drizzle with the sauce. Your guests will be very impressed!

1 oven plank, soaked in water for at least
   30 minutes
Artichoke Glaze (page 184)

4 thin lemon sole fillets, rinsed and patted dry
Herbed Tomato Vinaigrette (page 258)

Prepare an indirect fire in your grill (with heat on one side, no heat on the other). Place the fillets, skin-side up, on a flat surface and spread with the Artichoke Glaze. Starting from the widest end, roll up in a spiral. Place seam-side down on the baking plank and drizzle with half the vinaigrette. Place the plank on the indirect (no heat) side of the grill, close the lid, and cook for 45 minutes, or until the fish begins to flake when tested with a fork in the center. Serve right away with the remaining vinaigrette.

Serves 4

maple-planked cod & new potatoes with onion butter

see variations page 203

Tender white cod and a maple plank—a fresh taste of New England with all the flavor of a beachside supper. The Onion Butter keeps everything moist as it cooks on the plank.

for the onion butter
4 tbsp. sweet butter
1/2 cup chopped green onion
1/4 cup dry white wine
fine kosher or sea salt and freshly ground black
   pepper to taste

2 thin maple planks, soaked in water for at
   least 30 minutes
4 (6- to 8-oz.) cod fillets, rinsed and patted dry
1 pound new potatoes, scrubbed and quartered
chopped fresh Italian parsley, to garnish

Prepare an indirect fire in your grill (heat on one side, no heat on the other). Combine the butter, green onion, and wine in a food processor and pulse to blend. Season to taste. Place the cod on the soaked planks, then top with the potatoes. Season to taste. Dollop the butter mixture over the fish and potatoes. Place the planks on the indirect (no heat) side of the grill, close the lid, and cook for 45 minutes, or until the fish begins to flake when tested with a fork in the center and the potatoes are tender. Garnish with Italian parsley.

Serves 4

variations

planked shrimp with bistro butter

see base recipe page 179

planked scallops with bistro butter
Prepare the basic recipe, using sea scallops in place of shrimp.

planked shrimp with satay sauce
Prepare the basic recipe, using Satay Sauce (page 169) in place of Bistro Butter. Garnish with chopped fresh cilantro to serve.

planked shrimp rémoulade
Prepare the basic recipe, using Rémoulade (page 261) in place of Bistro Butter.

planked asian shrimp
Prepare the basic recipe, using Asian Vinaigrette (page 27) or 1/2 cup bottled teriyaki sauce in place of Bistro Butter.

planked salmon chimichurri

see base recipe page 180

planked salmon with tomato vinaigrette
Prepare the basic recipe, using Herbed Tomato Vinaigrette (page 258) in place of Chimichurri.

planked salmon rémoulade
Prepare the basic recipe, using Rémoulade (page 261) in place of Chimichurri.

planked ancho-buttered salmon
Prepare the basic recipe, using dollops of Ancho-Lime Butter (page 257) in place of Chimichurri. Top with 1 cup chopped fresh tomato, 1/2 cup chopped fresh cilantro, and 1/2 cup chopped green onion before grilling.

planked salmon with mustard dill aïoli
Prepare the basic recipe, replacing Chimichurri with Easy Aïoli (page 275), made with an additional 2 tablespoons Dijon mustard and 1 teaspoon dried dill weed. Top with fresh dill fronds before grilling.

variations

macadamia-buttered barramundi on a plank

see base recipe page 183

pistachio-buttered turbot on a plank
Prepare basic recipe, using skinless turbot fillets in place of barramundi, and roasted, chopped, shelled pistachios in place of macadamia nuts. Plank for 30 minutes or until turbot begins to flake when tested with a fork in the thickest part.

pecan-buttered walleye on a plank
Prepare basic recipe, using skinless walleye or other freshwater fillets in place of barramundi, and toasted chopped pecans in place of macadamias. Plank for 45 minutes or until walleye begins to flake when tested.

cilantro-buttered trout on a plank
Prepare basic recipe, using skinless trout or other freshwater fillets in place of barramundi, and 1/2 cup chopped cilantro in place of macadamias. Plank for 45 minutes or until trout flakes when tested.

orange-buttered sole on a plank
Prepare basic recipe, using skinless sole fillets in place of barramundi, and 1 teaspoon fresh orange zest and 1 teaspoon dried tarragon in place of macadamias. Plank for 30 minutes or until sole flakes when tested. Garnish with orange slices and tarragon sprigs.

alder-planked tilapia with artichoke glaze

see base recipe page 184

alder-planked tilapia with basil aïoli
Prepare the basic recipe, using Basil Aïoli in place of Artichoke Glaze. Make Easy Aïoli (page 275) and stir in 1/2 cup chopped fresh basil.

alder-planked tilapia with roasted red bell pepper glaze
Prepare the basic recipe, using drained and chopped canned roasted red bell peppers in place of artichokes in the glaze.

pesto-planked perch
Prepare the basic recipe, using 1/2 cup prepared pesto in place of Artichoke Glaze and ocean or lake perch fillets in place of tilapia. Serve with sliced fresh tomatoes.

harissa-planked hake with fresh salsa
Prepare the basic recipe, using 1/2 cup prepared harissa in place of Artichoke Glaze and hake fillets in place of tilapia. Serve with Mango & Lime Salsa (page 265) or Papaya & Lime Salsa (page 277) to cool off.

variations

planked monkfish tapa

see base recipe page 186

greek-style planked monkfish
Prepare the basic recipe, using 1/2 cup chopped Kalamata olives in place of
red bell pepper. Add 1/2 cup chopped, seeded cucumber and 1 teaspoon
dried oregano to the topping.

asian-style planked monkfish
Prepare the basic recipe, using 1/2 cup miso paste and 1/2 cup chopped
green onion in place of the topping.

provençal-style planked monkfish
Prepare the basic recipe, using 1/2 cup chopped fresh fennel in place of red
bell pepper and fresh lemon juice in place of vinegar. Add 1 teaspoon dried
tarragon to the topping.

mexican-style planked monkfish
Prepare the basic recipe, adding 1/4 cup chopped, seeded jalapeño pepper
and 1/2 cup chopped fresh tomato in place of red bell pepper, and fresh lime
juice in place of vinegar. Add 1 teaspoon ground cumin and 1 teaspoon
dried oregano to the topping.

tuna niçoise on a plank

see base recipe page 187

salmon niçoise on a plank
Prepare basic recipe, using 1 skinless salmon fillet in place of tuna steaks.
Cook for 45 minutes or until the fish flakes easily when tested with a fork in
the thickest part. Cut into 4 pieces to serve.

shrimp niçoise on a plank
Prepare basic recipe, using 1 pound peeled and deveined large shrimp in
place of tuna. Cook for 30 minutes or until they are pink and opaque.

grilled tuna niçoise
Prepare basic recipe, omitting the plank(s). Prepare a hot fire in the grill.
Steam the string beans until crisp-tender. Brush the tuna steaks with some
of the vinaigrette and grill for 2 minutes per side for rare.

grilled salmon niçoise
Prepare basic recipe, omitting the plank(s) and using a salmon fillet in place
of tuna steaks. Prepare a hot fire in your grill. Steam the string beans until
crisp-tender. Brush the salmon with some of the vinaigrette and grill for
3 1/2–4 minutes per side, turning once.

variations

planked mahi mahi with fresh pineapple salsa

see base recipe page 188

planked mahi mahi with fresh papaya salsa
Prepare the basic recipe, using Papaya & Lime Salsa (page 277) in place of Pineapple & Lime Salsa.

planked mahi mahi with fresh mango salsa
Prepare the basic recipe, using Mango & Lime Salsa (page 265) in place of Pineapple & Lime Salsa.

planked shrimp with fresh mango salsa
Prepare the basic recipe, using peeled and deveined jumbo shrimp in place of mahi mahi and Mango & Lime Salsa (page 265) in place of Pineapple & Lime Salsa. Cook for 30 minutes, or until the shrimp are pink and opaque.

planked scallops with fresh honeydew salsa
Prepare the basic recipe, using medium sea scallops in place of mahi mahi and Honeydew & Lime Salsa (page 277) in place of Pineapple & Lime Salsa. Cook for 30 minutes, or until the scallops are firm and opaque.

variations

smoke-planked lemon-tarragon snapper

see base recipe page 190

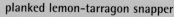

planked lemon-tarragon snapper
Prepare the basic recipe, but omit the wood chips.

smoke-planked lemon-tarragon scallops
Prepare the basic recipe, using 2 pounds medium sea scallops in place of snapper. Melt the Lemon-Tarragon Butter, toss the scallops in the mixture, then arrange on the planks. Cook for 30 minutes or until the scallops are firm and opaque.

smoke-planked lemon-tarragon shrimp
Prepare the basic recipe, using 2 pounds peeled and deveined large shrimp in place of snapper. Melt the Lemon-Tarragon Butter, toss the shrimp in the mixture, then arrange on the planks. Cook for 30 minutes or until the shrimp are pink and opaque.

smoke-planked lemon-tarragon salmon
Prepare the basic recipe, using salmon in place of snapper.

variations

cedar-planked sole roulade

see base recipe page 191

mediterranean sole roulade
Prepare the basic recipe, using 1/2 cup prepared pesto in place of the Artichoke Glaze.

roasted red bell pepper sole roulade
Prepare the basic recipe, using 1/2 cup Roasted Red Bell Pepper Puree (page 164) in place of the Artichoke Glaze.

provençal sole roulade
Prepare the basic recipe, using 1/2 cup prepared tapenade in place of the Artichoke Glaze.

planked sole roulade with basil aïoli
Prepare the basic recipe, using 1/2 cup Basil Aïoli (page 197) in place of the Artichoke Glaze.

maple-planked cod & new potatoes with onion butter

see base recipe page 192

maple-planked haddock with onion butter
Prepare the basic recipe, using haddock in place of cod.

maple-planked whitefish with three-pepper butter
Prepare the basic recipe, using whitefish in place of cod. Add 1/4 cup each chopped red, green, and yellow bell pepper to the Onion Butter and spread on the fish before planking.

maple-planked orange roughy with lemon-tarragon butter
Prepare the basic recipe, using orange roughy in place of cod and Lemon-Tarragon Butter (page 190) in place of Onion Butter.

maple-planked cod with tapas topping
Prepare the basic recipe, using Tapas Topping (page 186) in place of Onion Butter.

roasted

High heat roasting, like grilling over a hot fire, helps

seafood cook quickly to a crisp exterior and a moist

interior. While you're at it, why not roast a

vegetable along with it, then whip up an easy

sauce—and you've got dinner.

simple roasted shrimp & asparagus

see variations page 220

For an easy dinner or a platter-style appetizer, accompanied by a bowl or two of your favorite dipping sauces, this dish has no peer. For a sauce that goes with both roasted shrimp and asparagus, try Basil Aïoli (page 197), Sesame Mayonnaise (page 275), Asian Vinaigrette (page 27), or Satay Sauce (page 169). To snap off the tough end of the asparagus stalks, hold an end of each stalk in your hands and bend until the asparagus spear snaps. Discard the woody end.

1 lb. asparagus, woody ends snapped off
16–24 large shrimp, peeled and deveined
olive oil for tossing

fine kosher or sea salt and freshly ground black
  pepper to taste

Preheat the oven to 400°F. Place the asparagus in a large bowl, drizzle with olive oil, and toss to coat. Arrange the asparagus in one layer on a cookie sheet and season to taste. Roast for 10 minutes or until the asparagus is crisp-tender and browned.

Place the shrimp in a large bowl, drizzle with olive oil, and toss to coat. Arrange the shrimp in one layer on a large cookie sheet and season to taste. Roast for 5-6 minutes or until the shrimp are pink and opaque. Arrange the shrimp and asparagus on a large platter with a bowl of dipping sauce and serve hot or at room temperature.

Serves 4

oyster pan roast with buttery leeks

see variations page 221

Sip a buttery chardonnay while this dish roasts, then toast the good life. Serve this with crusty bread to mop up all the juices.

1 stick (4 oz.) sweet butter, melted
3 large leeks, trimmed, rinsed, and thinly sliced
2 pints fresh, shucked oysters, juices reserved

fine kosher or sea salt and coarsely ground
    black pepper to taste

Preheat the oven to 400°F. Place the butter and leeks in a large baking dish, stir to coat the leeks with butter, and roast for 5 minutes. Remove, pour in the reserved oyster juices, stir the leeks again, and return to the oven for another 10 minutes or until the leeks have softened. Remove from the oven and season to taste. Tuck the oysters under the leek mixture in the pan and return to the oven for another 10 minutes or until the edges of the oysters begin to curl. Serve in shallow pasta bowls or soup plates.

Serves 4

roasted baby octopus in sherry marinade

see variations page 222

Serve with a glass of chilled fino sherry to echo the marinade. Octopus needs high heat to cook quickly so it doesn't get rubbery, so it's best roasted or grilled.

for the sherry marinade
1/4 cup olive oil
1/4 cup dry sherry
6 garlic cloves, minced
1 tsp. paprika
1/2 tsp. fine kosher or sea salt

2 lbs. baby octopus, cleaned
8 fresh plum tomatoes, cut in half
1 cup pitted Kalamata or niçoise olives, cut in half
1/2 cup pimento-stuffed green olives, drained and diced
1/4 cup finely chopped fresh Italian parsley, to garnish

For the marinade, combine all the ingredients in a sealable plastic bag. Pour half the marinade into another container to reserve. Add the octopus to the marinade in the bag, seal, and marinate in the refrigerator for up to 12 hours.

Preheat the oven to 500°F. Arrange the tomatoes in a roasting pan and drizzle with a fourth of the reserved marinade. Roast the tomatoes for 10 minutes or until beginning to soften and brown. Remove the octopus from the marinade, do not pat dry, and place them with the tomatoes in the roasting pan. Return pan to the oven and roast for 3–5 minutes or until the octopus is white and opaque. Combine the octopus and tomatoes with the remaining reserved marinade and the olives. Portion onto plates and garnish with parsley.

Serves 8 as an appetizer

pecan-crusted catfish with roasted corn relish

see variations page 223

For a true taste of the Mississippi Delta, serve this colorful dish with cornbread.

for the roasted corn relish
2 cups fresh corn cut from the cob
1 cup cherry tomatoes, halved
1 cup chopped green or red bell pepper
1/2 cup chopped green onion
1/4 cup olive oil, plus more for drizzling
2 tbsp. red wine vinegar
fine kosher or sea salt and ground black pepper
    to taste

1 cup panko breadcrumbs
1/4 cup chopped pecans
1 tbsp. olive oil
2 tbsp. water
fine kosher or sea salt and ground black pepper
    to taste
4 skinless catfish fillets

Preheat the oven to 425°F. Place the corn, tomatoes, bell pepper, and onion in a large bowl, and toss with olive oil and vinegar to coat. Season to taste. Arrange the corn relish in one layer on a rimmed cookie sheet. In a small bowl, mix the breadcrumbs, pecans, 1 tablespoon olive oil, and water. Season to taste. Press the breadcrumb mixture onto the top of each catfish fillet. Arrange the catfish on the bed of corn relish, drizzle all with a little more olive oil, and roast for 10–12 minutes or until the catfish begins to flake when tested with a fork in the thickest part.

Serves 4

roasted monkfish romesco

see variations page 224

Serve this dish with crusty bread to mop up all the delicious juices. Colorful Romesco, a classic sauce from Catalonia, also functions as a vegetable in this dish.

for the romesco
1/2 cup almonds, toasted
1 slice white bread, toasted and crumbled
2 red bell peppers, roasted, seeded, and peeled
1 tbsp. chopped fresh Italian parsley
2 cloves garlic, minced
1/2 tsp. red pepper flakes
1/4 tsp. sea salt
1/4 tsp. freshly ground black pepper
1/3 cup red wine vinegar
2/3 cup extra-virgin olive oil

1 medium zucchini, thinly sliced into rounds
1 red onion, thinly sliced into rounds
olive oil for drizzling
fine kosher or sea salt and freshly ground black pepper to taste
4 skinless monkfish fillets

To make the sauce, finely grind the almonds in a food processor. Add the toasted bread, peppers, parsley, garlic, pepper flakes, salt, and pepper. Puree to form a smooth paste. Add the vinegar and blend. While the motor is running, slowly add the olive oil in a thin stream until all the ingredients are incorporated.

Preheat the oven to 425°F. Arrange the zucchini and onion slices on a cookie sheet, drizzle with olive oil, and season to taste. Place the fish fillets on the vegetables, drizzle with olive oil, and season to taste. Roast for 10–12 minutes or until the monkfish begins to flake when tested with a fork in the thickest part. Serve with Romesco.

Serves 4

jamaican roast turbot

see variations page 225

With distinctive jerk seasoning, these whole roast fish take on the flavor of the islands.
Scotch bonnet peppers are the hottest, so feel free to substitute jalapeño or serrano
peppers if your tastebuds can't take the heat. Dat good eat!

for the jerk seasoning
1 medium yellow onion, chopped
4 green onions, chopped
4 sprigs fresh thyme or 2 tsp. dried thyme
10 whole allspice berries
1 tbsp. fine kosher or sea salt
1 tbsp. ground black pepper

4 cloves garlic, minced
2 fresh scotch bonnet peppers, stemmed,
    seeded, and chopped
1/4 cup bottled pick-a-pepper sauce

4 small (about 1 lb. each) whole turbot,
    cleaned, with head and tail intact

Preheat the oven to 425°F. In a bowl, mix the jerk seasoning ingredients together.
Stuff each fish with the seasoning mixture, place the fish on a cookie sheet, and cover
with foil. Roast for 30–35 minutes or until the fish begins to flake when tested with a fork
in the thickest part.

Serves 4

pesce al forno

see variations page 226

Whole fish that are too small to grill, but too big to fry, work well with this traditional Italian oven method. They bake to a luscious, aromatic, crusty finish, so be sure to have lots of Italian bread to mop it all up.

1 1/2 lbs. whole, small fish, such as sardines, lake perch, smallmouth bass, or mackerel, with head and tail intact	4 tbsp. panko or other dried breadcrumbs
	1/4 cup finely chopped fresh Italian parsley
	1 tsp. dried oregano
5 tbsp. olive oil	1 tsp. grated lemon zest
2 bay leaves	1/2 cup dry white wine

Preheat the oven to 425°F. Cut the heads off the fish. Place each fish, cut-side down, on a flat surface and press down on fish with both hands to open like a book and flatten. With your fingers, remove the backbone, then cut off the tail. Drizzle 2 tablespoons of the olive oil in a baking dish and arrange the bay leaves on the bottom. Arrange the fish in dish, skin-side down, so that they fit snugly. In a bowl, combine remaining 3 tablespoons olive oil, breadcrumbs, parsley, oregano, and lemon zest. Sprinkle this mixture over the fish and pour in the wine. Roast for 18–20 minutes or until the fish begin to flake when tested with a fork in the thickest part.

Serves 8–10

tangy roast bluefish with coriander & bay

see variations page 227

Oily fish, such as bluefish and mackerel, benefit from a touch of vinegar and aromatic herbs, as in this recipe, which starts out in a cold oven.

3/4 stick (3 oz.) sweet butter, softened
20 bay leaves, snipped with scissors
2 tbsp. whole coriander seeds
2 tbsp. coarse sea or kosher salt
1 (4-lb.) whole bluefish, cleaned, with head and
    tail intact

1 lemon, thinly sliced
1 cup tarragon vinegar
6 whole black peppercorns
fine sea salt to taste

Spread 2 tablespoons of the butter over the bottom of a roasting pan. In a bowl, combine the remaining butter, bay leaves, coriander seeds, and salt. Spread the interior of the fish with half of the flavored butter, then stuff with lemon slices. Place the fish diagonally in the roasting pan, turning the tail up and over if necessary to fit. Dot the fish with the remaining flavored butter. Place in a cold oven and turn the temperature to 500°F. Roast for 40–45 minutes or until the fish begins to flake when tested with a fork in the thickest part.

Transfer the fish to a serving platter and tent with foil. Pour the juices from the roasting pan into a large saucepan over high heat. Stir in the vinegar, peppercorns, and sea salt, and bring to a boil for 1 minute. Pour the hot sauce over the fish and serve.

Serves 4–6

basque-style roast fish

see variations page 228

From the Pyrenees to the Cantabrian Mountains, the Basque people prefer the wild mountains. Their unique cuisine makes the most of the lamb they raise as well as the fish they catch.

1/4 cup olive oil
2 medium onions, chopped
2 cloves garlic, minced
1 (4-oz.) can sliced pimentos
1 cup chopped fresh or canned tomatoes, drained

1 tsp. smoked or Hungarian paprika
1/2 cup chopped fresh Italian parsley
4 whole, small rainbow trout, cleaned, heads and tails removed
1/2 cup dry white wine

Preheat the oven to 425°F. In a bowl, mix the olive oil, onions, garlic, pimentos, tomatoes, paprika, and parsley together. Stuff each fish with the mixture, place the fish in a large, oiled baking dish, pour in the wine, and cover with foil. Roast for 30–35 minutes or until the fish begins to flake when tested with a fork in the thickest part.

Serves 4

korean roasted branzino

see variations page 229

Branzino, or European sea bass, is delicious when roasted. Prepared kimchee is a spicy Korean cabbage relish that is available in better grocery stores.

4 (6-to 8-oz.) branzino fillets, rinsed and
    patted dry
2 cups prepared kimchee, coarsely chopped
for the korean kochukaru sauce
1/4 cup soy sauce
1 tbsp. sugar

1 tbsp. rice wine
2 tsp. sesame oil
2 tbsp. kochukaru (Korean chili pepper flakes)
fine kosher or sea salt and freshly ground black
    pepper to taste

Preheat the oven to 425°F. Arrange the fillets on an oiled cookie sheet and top with the kimchee. Roast for 20–25 minutes or until the fish begins to flake when tested with a fork in the thickest part. In a saucepan, bring the soy sauce, sugar, and rice wine to a boil. Stir to dissolve the sugar. Remove from the heat and stir in the sesame oil and chili pepper flakes. Season to taste. Pour sauce over the fish and serve.

Serves 4

simple roasted shrimp & asparagus

see base recipe page 205

creole roasted shrimp & pepper po' boy
Prepare basic recipe, seasoning shrimp with Creole-style seasoning. Roast a red, yellow, and green bell pepper, seeded and cut into strips, in place of asparagus. Spread 4 hoagie or French rolls with Rémoulade (page 261). Divide roasted shrimp and peppers among the rolls, and top with shredded lettuce and sliced tomato to make a sandwich.

simple roasted shrimp & asparagus with orange hollandaise
Prepare basic recipe. Serve with Orange Hollandaise (page 276).

simple roasted scallops & asparagus
Prepare basic recipe, using medium sea scallops in place of shrimp. Roast for 5–6 minutes or until they are almost opaque and firm to the touch.

roasted chipotle shrimp bruschetta
Prepare basic recipe, omitting asparagus. Mix 1/4 cup canned squash puree, 1/4 cup fresh goat cheese, 1 finely chopped, canned chipotle pepper in adobo sauce, 1 tablespoon honey, and 1 tablespoon cider vinegar until well blended. Spread on toasted bread, top with roasted shrimp, and garnish with chopped cilantro.

variations

oyster pan roast with buttery leeks

see base recipe page 206

buttery oyster leek penne
Prepare the basic recipe, using very small oysters. Bring a large pot of salted water to a boil and cook 1 pound of penne until al dente. Drain and toss with the oyster pan roast and garnish with freshly grated Parmesan.

oyster pan roast with buttery leeks & new potatoes
Prepare the basic recipe, adding 8 ounces new potatoes, scrubbed and quartered, to the leek mixture before roasting.

oyster & leek chowder
Prepare the basic recipe. Stir 2 cups prepared Alfredo sauce into the roasted leek mixture, tuck the oysters under the leeks, then return to the oven until the edges of the oysters have curled and the soup is hot. Ladle into bowls and serve with oyster crackers.

pan-roasted shrimp with buttery leeks
Prepare the basic recipe, using 1/2 cup dry white wine in place of oyster juices and 1 pound peeled and deveined large shrimp in place of oysters.

variations

roasted baby octopus in sherry marinade

see base recipe page 209

roasted baby cuttlefish in sherry marinade
Prepare the basic recipe, using baby cuttlefish in place of octopus.

roasted baby squid in sherry marinade
Prepare the basic recipe, using baby squid, heads removed, in place
of octopus.

roasted shrimp in sherry marinade
Prepare the basic recipe, using peeled and deveined large shrimp in place
of octopus. Roast for 5–7 minutes or until the shrimp turn pink and opaque.

roasted scallops in sherry marinade
Prepare the basic recipe, using medium sea scallops in place of octopus. Add
1 cup chopped zucchini and 1 coarsely chopped red onion, drizzled with
olive oil and seasoned to taste, to the tomatoes before roasting them.

variations

pecan-crusted catfish with roasted corn relish

see base recipe page 210

roasted pecan-crusted tilapia with basil aïoli
Prepare the basic recipe, omitting the corn relish, and serve topped with
Basil Aïoli (page 197).

roasted almond-crusted salmon with roasted corn relish
Prepare the basic recipe, using salmon in place of catfish and chopped
almonds in place of pecans.

roasted halibut with roasted red bell pepper relish
Prepare the basic recipe, using halibut in place of catfish and chopped red
bell pepper in place of corn.

roasted hake with artichoke glaze
Prepare the basic recipe, using hake fillets in place of catfish and Artichoke
Glaze (page 184) in place of the breadcrumb-pecan topping.

variations

roasted monkfish with romesco

see base recipe page 212

roasted shrimp with romesco
Prepare the basic recipe, using peeled and deveined large shrimp in place of monkfish. Roast for 8–10 minutes or until the shrimp are pink and opaque.

roasted halibut with romesco
Prepare the basic recipe, using halibut in place of monkfish.

roasted monkfish soup with rouille
Prepare the basic recipe, using Rouille (page 275) in place of Romesco. Serve the roasted vegetables and fish in shallow bowls, topped with hot prepared fish stock. Dollop with the Rouille.

roasted monkfish & shrimp soup with rouille
Prepare the basic recipe, using half monkfish and half peeled and deveined large shrimp and Rouille (page 275) in place of Romesco. Roast for 8–10 minutes or until the shrimp are pink and opaque. Serve the roasted vegetables and seafood in shallow bowls, topped with hot fish stock. Dollop with the Rouille.

variations

jamaican roast turbot

see base recipe page 213

spanish roast turbot in sherry marinade
Prepare basic recipe, omitting jerk seasoning. Make a stuffing with
Sherry Marinade (page 209), 1 cup chopped pitted Kalamata olives, and 1
cup chopped pimento-stuffed green olives. Stuff each fish, cover, and roast.

french roast turbot
Prepare basic recipe, omitting jerk seasoning. Stuff each fish with 4 sprigs
tarragon, 4 lemon slices, salt, and pepper, then drizzle inside and out with
1 tablespoon melted butter. Cover and roast.

roast turbot with parsley sauce
Prepare the basic recipe, omitting jerk seasoning. Stuff each fish with
4 sprigs Italian parsley, 4 lemon slices, salt, and pepper, then drizzle inside
and out with 1 tablespoon melted butter. Cover and roast. Warm 2 cups
prepared Alfredo sauce and stir in 1/2 cup chopped fresh Italian parsley.
Serve with roast fish.

roasted jerk salmon
Prepare basic recipe, using a whole salmon fillet spread with jerk seasoning.
Cover and roast for 20 minutes or until the fish begins to flake when tested
with a fork in the thickest part.

variations

pesce al forno

see base recipe page 214

italian roast fish fillets
Prepare the basic recipe, using 1 1/2 pounds fish fillets in place of small whole fish. Roast for 10–12 minutes or until the fish begins to flake when tested with a fork in the thickest part.

italian roast shrimp
Prepare the basic recipe, using 1 1/2 pounds whole, large shrimp, peeled and deveined, in place of fish. Roast for 8–10 minutes or until the shrimp are pink and opaque.

venetian roast lobster
Prepare the basic recipe, using 4 rock lobster tails. Have your fishmonger dispatch live lobster and cut the lobster tails for you; do not butterfly. Arrange them in the dish with the other ingredients. Roast for 10–12 minutes, or until the lobster meat is white and opaque, and the shells are red.

italian roast large fish
Prepare the basic recipe, using 1 large whole fish in place of the small fish. Roast for 20–22 minutes or until the fish begins to flake when tested with a fork in the thickest part.

variations

tangy roast bluefish with coriander & bay

see base recipe page 216

tangy roast mackerel with coriander & bay
Prepare the basic recipe, using mackerel in place of bluefish.

tangy roast sardines with coriander & bay
Prepare the basic recipe, using large sardines in place of bluefish. Roast for 30–35 minutes or until the sardines flake when tested with a fork in the thickest part.

roast amberjack in sherry marinade
Instead of the basic recipe, use Sherry Marinade (page 209) and amberjack in place of bluefish. Brush the fish, inside and out with the marinade, then pour the rest of it around the fish. Roast for 30–35 minutes or until the fish begins to flake when tested with a fork in the thickest part.

tangy roast kingfish with coriander & bay
Prepare the basic recipe, using kingfish in place of bluefish.

variations

basque-style roast fish

see base recipe page 217

bacon-wrapped roast trout
Prepare the basic recipe, wrapping each trout with a slice of bacon, before cooking. Remove the foil during the last 10 minutes of cooking to crisp the bacon.

tapas-style roast fish
Prepare the basic recipe, using Tapas Topping (page 186) to stuff the fish in place of the olive oil, onions, garlic, tomatoes, pimentos, and parsley.

asian roast trout
Prepare the basic recipe, using a mixture of 1/2 cup chopped green onion, 1/2 cup fermented black beans, and 2 tablespoons grated fresh gingerroot to stuff the fish in place of the olive oil, onions, garlic, tomatoes, pimentos, and parsley. Use sake or rice wine in place of dry white wine.

easy mexican roast trout
Prepare the basic recipe, using 2 cups fresh prepared tomato salsa to stuff the fish in place of the olive oil, onions, garlic, tomatoes, pimentos, and parsley. Use tequila in place of dry white wine.

korean roasted branzino

see base recipe page 218

korean branzino en papillote
Prepare the basic recipe, but instead of the baking pan, place each fillet on a 16-inch square of parchment paper before topping with kimchee, and wrap like a parcel. Roast for 20 minutes. Pass the sauce at the table.

oven-roasted whitefish with three-pepper butter
Prepare the basic recipe, using whitefish in place of branzino and omitting sauce. But instead of the baking pan, place each fillet on a 16-inch square of parchment paper. Add 1/4 cup each chopped red, green, and yellow bell pepper to prepared Onion Butter (page 192). Spread on the fish and wrap like a parcel before roasting.

roasted orange roughy with lemon-tarragon butter
Prepare the basic recipe, using orange roughy in place of branzino and Lemon-Tarragon Butter (page 190) in place of kimchee. Omit the sauce.

roasted branzino with tapas topping
Prepare the basic recipe, using Tapas Topping (page 186) in place of kimchee. Omit the sauce.

in the smoker

For centuries, fish and shellfish were salted and dried or smoked to preserve them during the cold months when fishing was too perilous. Today, we love smoked seafood because it tastes so wonderful, and in so many ways—from center-of-the-plate fillets to the smoky heart of soups, stews, and savory dips.

leaf-wrapped smoked shrimp with rémoulade

see variations page 246

The classic shrimp cocktail just got a lot more interesting!

24 large shrimp, peeled and deveined, rinsed
and patted dry
24 fresh baby spinach leaves, rinsed, and
patted dry
olive oil for brushing
fine kosher or sea salt to taste

6 (12-inch) bamboo skewers, soaked in water
for 30 minutes
1 cup dry wood chips, such as mesquite,
hickory, or alder
Rémoulade (page 261), to serve

Prepare an indirect fire in your grill (with a fire on one side and no fire on the other). Wrap each shrimp around the middle in a spinach leaf and thread onto the soaked wooden skewers. Brush with olive oil, and season with salt. For a charcoal grill, throw the dry wood chips on the coals. For a gas grill, make a packet out of aluminum foil to contain the chips, poke holes in the packet, and place by a gas burner. Place the skewers on the indirect (no heat) side of the grill. When you see the first wisp of smoke, close the lid. Smoke for 20–30 minutes or until the shrimp have a burnished pink appearance and are opaque. Serve with the Rémoulade.

Serves 6

smoked oyster po' boy sandwich

see variations page 247

Oysters take on a more complex flavor when they're hot-smoked. Use larger varieties like Blue Point or Kumamoto for this recipe.

12 shucked oysters, rinsed and patted dry
olive oil for brushing
fine kosher or sea salt
1 cup dry wood chips, such as mesquite,
    hickory, or alder

4 hoagie rolls or hot dog buns
Rémoulade (261)
2 cups shredded lettuce
2 fresh tomatoes, thinly sliced

Prepare an indirect fire in your grill (a fire on one side and no fire on the other). Brush the oysters with olive oil, season with salt, and place in a disposable aluminum pan. For a charcoal grill, throw the dry wood chips on the coals. For a gas grill, make a packet out of aluminum foil to hold the chips, poke holes in the packet, and place by a gas burner. Place the oyster pan on the indirect (no heat) side of the grill. When you see the first wisp of smoke, close the lid. Smoke for 20–30 minutes or until the oysters have a burnished appearance and the edges have curled. Split and toast the hoagie rolls on the hot side of the grill. Spread the inside of the rolls with Rémoulade. Top the bottom roll with shredded lettuce and thinly sliced tomatoes. Arrange the hot oysters on top of the tomatoes, replace the top bun, and serve.

Serves 4

smoked scallops with tomato-spinach orzo

see variations page 248

The slight bitterness from wood smoke makes a fine counterpoint to the natural sweetness of scallops. Serve them on a bed of colorful pasta that is both sauce and side dish.

12 large sea scallops, rinsed and patted dry
olive oil for brushing
fine kosher or sea salt to tasate

1 cup dry wood chips, such as mesquite,
hickory, or alder
Tomato-Spinach Orzo (page 268), to serve

Prepare an indirect fire in your grill (a fire on one side and no fire on the other). Brush the oysters with olive oil, season with salt, and place in a disposable aluminum pan. For a charcoal grill, throw the dry wood chips on the coals. For a gas grill, make a packet out of aluminum foil to contain the chips, poke holes in the packet, and place by a gas burner. Place the oysters on the indirect (no heat) side of the grill. When you see the first wisp of smoke, close the lid. Smoke for 20–30 minutes or until the scallops have a burnished appearance and are opaque. Serve the scallops atop Tomato-Spinach Orzo.

Serves 4

smoked mussels with frites & aïoli

see variations page 249

In this new take on the classic Belgian dish of steamed mussels paired with crisp French fries and homemade mayonnaise, you both smoke and grill the mussels over high heat, so they open. Make sure you scrub away the "beard" from each mussel. Discard any that are open before you smoke them as well as any that don't open after smoking.

3 lbs. mussels, scrubbed, with beards removed
1 cup dry wood chips, such as mesquite,
   hickory, or alder
1/4 cup chopped fresh Italian parsley, to garnish

Frites (page 269), to serve
Aïoli (page 262), to serve

Prepare an indirect fire in your grill (a fire on one side and no fire on the other). Place the mussels in a disposable aluminum pan. For a charcoal grill, throw the dry wood chips on the coals. For a gas grill, make a packet out of aluminum foil to hold the chips, poke holes in the packet, and place by a gas burner. Place the oysters on the direct (high heat) side of the grill. When you see the first wisp of smoke, close the lid. Smoke for 10–15 minutes or until the mussels have opened and have a smoky aroma. Serve the mussels, garnished with parsley, in bowls accompanied by Frites and Aïoli.

Serves 4

apple-smoked salmon

see variations page 250

A grill-smoked salmon fillet, served on a platter, can be the eye-catching centerpiece of a brunch, lunch, or casual get-together. This looks wonderful on a platter, garnished with thinly sliced lemons and fresh dill sprigs.

1 (1 1/2 to 2 lb.) boneless, skinless salmon fillet
1 (12-oz.) bottle zesty Italian dressing

1/2 cup Cajun-style seafood seasoning or dry rub of your choice
1 cup dry wood chips, such as apple

Place the salmon fillet in a plastic container or zipper-top plastic bag. Pour the Italian dressing into the bag. Cover and marinate the fillet for 3–4 hours in the refrigerator. Remove the salmon from the marinade (do not pat dry) and discard the marinade. Sprinkle the seasoning or dry rub on the top of the fish.

Prepare an indirect fire in your grill (a fire on one side and no fire on the other). For a charcoal grill, throw the dry wood chips on the coals. For a gas grill, make a packet out of aluminum foil to hold the chips, poke holes in the packet, and place by a gas burner. Place the salmon on the indirect (no heat) side of the grill. When you see the first wisp of smoke, close the lid. Smoke for 45–60 minutes or until the salmon is burnished, has a smoky aroma, and begins to flake when tested with a fork in the thickest part. Serve on a platter, garnished as desired, and use leftover salmon in any of the recipe variations on page 250.

Serves 8

smoked trout with fresh herb butter

see variations page 251

Hot smoked trout is fabulous. It has a smoky aroma, a delicate and moist texture, and fabulous flavor. It looks wonderful when garnished with thinly sliced lemons and sprigs of fresh herbs. Use any leftovers in pâté, for breakfast with eggs, or in sandwiches.

4 (12- to 16-oz.) whole trout, dressed, rinsed, and patted dry
Fresh Herb Butter (page 272)

1 cup dry wood chips, such as hickory, oak, or pecan

Open each trout like a book and spread with some of the herb butter, inside and out. Prepare an indirect fire in your grill (a fire on one side and no fire on the other). For a charcoal grill, throw the dry wood chips on the coals. For a gas grill, make a packet out of aluminum foil to contain the chips, poke holes in the packet, and place by a gas burner. Place the trout on the indirect (no heat) side of the grill. When you see the first wisp of smoke, close the lid. Smoke for 45–60 minutes or until the trout are burnished, have a smoky aroma, and begin to flake when tested with a fork in the thickest part. Serve on a platter, garnished as desired, and use leftovers in variations on page 251.

Serves 4

maple-smoked whitefish with butternut squash, sage & parmesan orzo

see variations page 252

Fisheries around the Great Lakes sell lots of fresh whitefish, lake perch, and chubs in good weather. They also smoke their catch for winter use, using local maple hardwood. You can do the same on your grill. Serve the succulent whitefish with another cold weather dish, Butternut Squash, Sage & Parmesan Orzo.

4 (6- to 8-oz.) whitefish fillets, rinsed and patted dry
canola oil for brushing
fine kosher or sea salt and ground black pepper to taste

1 cup dry wood chips, such as hickory, oak, or pecan
Butternut Squash, Sage & Parmesan Orzo (page 279), to serve

Brush the fish with oil and season to taste. Oil a perforated grill rack or disposable aluminum cookie sheet and place the fish on it. Prepare an indirect fire in your grill (a fire on one side and no fire on the other). For a charcoal grill, throw the dry wood chips on the coals. For a gas grill, make a packet out of aluminum foil to hold the chips, poke holes in the packet, and place by a gas burner. Place the fish on the indirect (no heat) side of the grill. At the first wisp of smoke, close the lid. Smoke for 15–20 minutes or until the fish is burnished, has a smoky aroma, and begins to flake when tested with a fork in the thickest part. Serve with the Orzo.

Serves 8–10

smoked haddock with hollandaise

see variations page 253

Known as "finnan haddie" in Scotland, smoked haddock is usually cold-smoked. This hot-smoked version, paired with luscious Hollandaise (page 264), mimics a classic French dish served at brasseries along the Atlantic coast.

4 haddock fillets, rinsed and patted dry
olive oil for brushing
fine kosher or sea salt and freshly ground black
    pepper to taste

1 cup dry wood chips, such as hickory, oak,
    or pecan
Blender Hollandaise (page 264)

Brush the fish with oil and season to taste. Oil a perforated grill rack or disposable aluminum cookie sheet and place the fish on it. Prepare an indirect fire in your grill (a fire on one side and no fire on the other). For a charcoal grill, throw the dry wood chips on the coals. For a gas grill, make a packet out of aluminum foil to contain the chips, poke holes in the packet, and place by a gas burner. Place the fish on the indirect (no heat) side of the grill. When you see the first wisp of smoke, close the lid. Smoke for 20–30 minutes or until the fish is burnished, has a smoky aroma, and begins to flake when tested with a fork in the thickest part. To serve, spoon the Hollandaise over each fillet.

Serves 4

cape kedgeree

see variations page 254

Kedgeree, dating from British colonial days, is a brunch dish made with flaked, smoked fish, cooked rice, hard-boiled eggs, fresh herbs, and a white sauce to bind it all together. Some people like to add a dash of curry powder. When made with hot-smoked fish, this dish is divine. Although smoked haddock is the usual fish for kedgeree, you can also use salmon, trout, or whitefish.

3 tbsp. butter
1 tbsp. chopped onion
3 tbsp. all-purpose flour
2 cups milk
1 tsp. curry powder (optional)
2 cups flaked, smoked haddock (page 242)

2 large eggs, hard-boiled and finely chopped
2 cups cooked white rice
1/2 cup chopped fresh Italian parsley
fine kosher or sea salt and freshly ground black
     pepper to taste

Melt the butter in a large saucepan over medium-high heat, then sauté the onion until transparent, about 4 minutes. Stir in the flour and cook, stirring, for 2 minutes. Whisk in the milk and cook, whisking constantly, until the sauce thickens, about 5 minutes. Stir in the optional curry powder, haddock, eggs, rice, and parsley until well combined. Season to taste and serve hot.

Serves 4

bayou smoked catfish 'n' corn

see variations page 255

This Mississippi Delta recipe is easy to do. Fire up your grill. Slice the kernels off ears of fresh uncooked corn so they stay together in "planks." Brush the corn and fish with oil and season with Cajun spices. Then smoke to a burnished goodness.

4 catfish fillets, rinsed and patted dry
4 ears fresh corn, the kernels sliced off with a
    sharp knife in "planks"

1/4 cup olive oil
1 tbsp. Cajun seasoning or to taste

Brush the fish and corn with oil and season to taste. Oil a perforated grill rack or disposable aluminum cookie sheet and place the fish and corn on it. Prepare an indirect fire in your grill (a fire on one side and no fire on the other). For a charcoal grill, throw the dry wood chips on the coals. For a gas grill, make a packet out of aluminum foil to hold the chips, poke holes in the packet, and place by a gas burner. Place the fish on the indirect (no heat) side of the grill. When you see the first wisp of smoke, close the lid. Smoke for 20–30 minutes or until the fish is burnished, has a smoky aroma, and begins to flake when tested with a fork in the thickest part.

Serves 4

variations

leaf-wrapped smoked shrimp with rémoulade

see base recipe page 231

leaf-wrapped stovetop-smoked shrimp with rémoulade
Prepare basic recipe, using a stovetop smoker. Place 1 rounded tablespoonful of fine, dry wood chips in the center of the bottom of smoker. Cover with the deflector pan, then the rack. Place skewers on rack and slide cover almost closed. Place smoker over medium-high heat. At the first wisp of smoke, close the lid all the way. Smoke for 8 minutes or until shrimp are burnished pink and opaque.

leaf-wrapped smoked shrimp with tarragon hollandaise
Prepare basic recipe, using Tarragon Hollandaise (page 276) in place of Rémoulade.

leaf-wrapped smoked shrimp with cocktail sauce
Prepare basic recipe, using Classic Cocktail Sauce (page 49) in place of Rémoulade.

open-face smoked shrimp sandwiches with tarragon hollandaise
Prepare basic recipe, omitting Rémoulade. Brush 4 slices of country bread, then grill on both sides to get good grill marks. Top with smoked shrimp. Combine 1/2 cup chopped fresh tomato, 1/2 cup chopped pitted Kalamata olives, and 2 tablespoons capers. Top shrimp with Tarragon Hollandaise (page 276), then some tomato mixture.

variations

smoked oyster po' boy sandwich

see base recipe page 232

smoked shrimp po' boy sandwich
Prepare basic recipe, using 24 smoked shrimp in place of oysters.

smoked scallop po' boy sandwich
Prepare basic recipe, using 12 smoked sea scallops in place of oysters.

stovetop-smoked oysters
Prepare basic recipe, using a stovetop smoker in place of a grill. Place
1 rounded tablespoonful of fine, dry wood chips in the center of the bottom
of the stovetop smoker. Cover with the deflector pan, then the rack. Place
oysters on the rack and slide the cover almost closed. Place smoker over
medium-high heat. At the first wisp of smoke, close the lid all the way.
Smoke for 8 minutes or until oysters are burnished and opaque.

smoked oyster stew
Prepare basic recipe. Add smoked oysters to Oyster Stew (page 84), replacing
1 dozen fresh oysters, during the last 5 minutes of cooking.

variations

smoked scallops with tomato-spinach orzo

see base recipe page 235

smoked scallops with mango salsa
Prepare basic recipe, using Mango & Lime Salsa (page 265) in place of Orzo.

stovetop-smoked scallops with tomato-spinach orzo
Prepare basic recipe, using a stovetop smoker in place of a grill. Place 1 rounded tablespoonful of fine, dry wood chips in the center of the smoker's bottom. Cover with the deflector pan, then the rack. Place the oysters on the rack and slide the cover almost closed. Place the smoker over medium-high heat. When you see the first wisp of smoke, close the lid all the way. Smoke for 8 minutes or until the scallops are burnished and opaque.

smoked scallop pasta with bistro butter
Prepare basic recipe, using 1 pound bay scallops in place of sea scallops. Smoke for 15 minutes. Toss the smoked scallops with 1 pound cooked penne and Bistro Butter (page 272) in place of Orzo.

smoked scallop chowder
Prepare basic recipe, using 1 pound bay scallops in place of sea scallops. Smoke for 15 minutes. Add scallops in place of clams in Clam Chowder (page 76).

variations

smoked mussels with frites & aïoli

see base recipe page 236

smoked mussels vinaigrette
Prepare the basic recipe, omitting the Frites and Aïoli. Remove the mussels from the shells and toss with Herbed Tomato Vinaigrette (page 258). Serve over baby greens.

smoked mussels with grilled bread & ancho butter
Prepare the basic recipe, omitting the Frites and Aïoli. Brush slices of country bread with Ancho-Lime Butter (page 257), grill on both sides for good grill marks, and serve with mussels.

smoked mussel chowder
Prepare the basic recipe, omitting the Frites and Aïoli. Remove the mussels from the shells and add to Clam Chowder (page 76), in place of clams, during the last 5 minutes of cooking.

smoked mussel pasta with basil aïoli
Prepare the basic recipe, omitting the Frites. Remove the mussels from the shells. Toss the smoked mussels with 1 pound cooked penne and Basil Aïoli (page 197).

apple-smoked salmon

see base recipe page 238

apple-smoked salmon pâté

Prepare basic recipe. In a food processor, process 1 cup flaked smoked salmon (about 4 ounces), 1/2 cup softened sweet butter, 1 tablespoon chopped fresh dill, and 1 teaspoon grated lemon zest until smooth. Serve the pâté in a crock, garnished with more chopped fresh dill and surrounded with sesame crackers or slices of French or pumpernickel bread.

smoked salmon cakes

Prepare basic recipe. Use leftover salmon in place of crabmeat in basic Crab Cakes (page 105).

smoked salmon aïoli salad

Prepare basic recipe. Place the smoked salmon atop 4 cups greens on a platter. Serve a bowl of Aïoli on the side. (page 262).

smoked salmon scrambled eggs

Prepare basic recipe. Whisk 6 large eggs with 2 tablespoons cream, 2 tablespoons snipped fresh chives, and salt and pepper to taste. Melt 1 tablespoon butter in a large, nonstick skillet. Add egg mixture and 1 cup flaked, smoked salmon fillet. Cook until softly scrambled. Garnish with more snipped chives and sour cream.

variations

smoked trout with fresh herb butter

see base recipe page 239

smoked trout scrambled eggs
Prepare basic recipe. Whisk 6 large eggs with 2 tablespoons cream,
2 tablespoons snipped fresh chives, salt, and pepper. Melt 1 tablespoon
butter in large skillet. Add egg mixture and 1 cup flaked, smoked trout, and
softly scramble. Garnish with snipped chives and sour cream.

smoked trout salad
Prepare basic recipe. Serve smoked trout fillets over baby greens and
steamed new potatoes. Drizzle with Lemon-Dill Vinaigrette (page 273)
before serving.

smoked trout pâté
Prepare basic recipe. Place 1 cup flaked smoked trout (about 4 ounces) in a
food processor. Add 1/2 cup softened sweet butter, 1 tablespoon chopped
fresh dill, and 1 teaspoon grated lemon zest. Process until smooth. Serve
pâté, garnished with fresh dill, in a crock with sesame crackers or slices of
French or pumpernickel bread.

smoked trout with horseradish cream
Prepare basic recipe. Chill leftover fillets and serve on baby greens. Dollop
with mixture of 1/2 cup sour cream, 1/2 cup heavy cream, and prepared
horseradish to taste.

maple-smoked whitefish with butternut squash, sage & parmesan orzo

see base recipe page 240

maple-smoked whitefish beignets
Prepare the basic recipe, omitting the Orzo. Use the maple-smoked whitefish in place of fresh whitefish in the basic Whitefish Beignets recipe (page 102).

maple-smoked whitefish & wild rice salad
Prepare the basic recipe, omitting the Orzo. Flake 1 cup of the fish and combine it with 1 cup cooked wild rice, 1 cup mayonnaise, 1/2 cup chopped green onion, 1/2 cup toasted pecans, and salt and ground white pepper to taste.

maple-smoked whitefish soup
Prepare the basic recipe. Combine 1 cup flaked, leftover whitefish with 1 cup leftover Orzo and 2 cups chicken broth. Bring to a simmer and serve hot.

maple-smoked walleye pike with butternut squash, sage & parmesan orzo
Prepare the basic recipe, using walleye pike in place of whitefish.

variations

smoked haddock with hollandaise

see base recipe page 242

smoked haddock with orange hollandaise
Prepare the basic recipe, using Orange Hollandaise (page 276) in place of
Blender Hollandaise.

smoked cod with hollandaise
Prepare the basic recipe, using cod in place of haddock.

prosciutto-wrapped haddock
Prepare the basic recipe, wrapping each fillet with a piece of prosciutto and
securing with a toothpick before smoking.

smoked haddock with roasted red bell pepper & basil puree
Prepare the basic recipe, serving each fillet over Roasted Red Bell Pepper &
Basil Puree (page 164).

variations

cape kedgeree

see base recipe page 243

cape kedgeree with apple-smoked salmon
Prepare the basic recipe, using apple-smoked salmon (page 238) in place of the haddock.

cape kedgeree with maple-smoked whitefish
Prepare the basic recipe, using maple-smoked whitefish (page 240) in place of the haddock.

kedgeree cakes
Prepare the basic recipe. The next day, take any leftover kedgeree and form the mixture into cakes. Dip in beaten egg, then in all-purpose flour, and fry in butter until browned on both sides.

kedgeree-stuffed tomatoes
Prepare the basic recipe. Stem and remove half of the interiors of 8 ripe, large tomatoes. Fill with the kedgeree, garnish with parsley, and serve hot or cold.

bayou smoked catfish 'n' corn

see base recipe page 244

hot smoked catfish dip
Prepare basic recipe, omitting corn. Prepare Classic Crab Dip (page 127), using 2 cups smoked catfish in place of crab.

low-country smoked catfish & rice
Prepare basic recipe, omitting corn. Flake 2 cups of fish and use in place of haddock in Cape Kedgeree (page 243). Use Cajun seasoning in place of curry powder.

bayou smoked catfish 'n' corn salad
Prepare basic recipe. Flake 1 cup of catfish and combine with 1 cup smoked corn, 1 cup mayonnaise, 1/2 cup chopped green onions, 1/2 cup chopped red bell pepper, and salt and ground white pepper to taste. Serve right away or cover and chill.

bayou smoked catfish 'n' corn soup
Prepare basic recipe. Flake 1 cup of catfish. Stir into 4 cups boiling chicken broth with 1 cup smoked corn; 1 cup chopped, cooked andouille or chorizo sausage; and 1 cup chopped canned tomatoes. Simmer for 15 minutes, then taste for seasoning. Serve garnished with chopped green onions.

sauces & sides

Some things just naturally go with the delicate or briny flavor of seafood. From the classic hollandaise and flavored butters to coleslaw and salsas, seafood meals just taste better with their accompaniments.

ancho-lime butter

see variations page 272

This delicious compound butter goes well with any grilled fish or shellfish. Place a pat or dollop of it on seafood when it's hot off the grill.

2 sticks (8 oz.) sweet butter, room temperature
1 tsp. ground ancho
1/4 cup chopped fresh cilantro leaves

1 clove garlic, minced
2 tsp. fresh lime juice

In a bowl, combine all the ingredients. Serve immediately or roll into a log and wrap in plastic wrap. It will keep, refrigerated, for about a week. Frozen and wrapped in additional freezer plastic wrap, the butter will keep for about 3 months.

Makes about 1 cup

herbed tomato vinaigrette

see variations page 273

Use full-flavored vinaigrettes like this one to drizzle over any cooked fish or shellfish.
Finish the dish with a sprinkling of fresh herbs or baby greens.

2 cups coarsely chopped fresh or canned plum
    tomatoes, drained
1/2 cup fresh Italian parsley
1/4 cup fresh cilantro
1/4 cup fresh mint
2 tbsp. fresh oregano
1/4 cup chopped yellow onion

3 peeled garlic cloves
1/2 tsp. cayenne pepper
1 tsp. fine kosher or sea salt
1 tsp. freshly ground black pepper
1/3 cup olive oil
1/3 cup sherry vinegar
1/4 cup water

Place all ingredients in a food processor and process until smooth. (The vinaigrette is best
served the same day but will keep, covered, in the refrigerator for up to 5 days.)

Makes about 2 cups

rémoulade

see variations page 274

Rémoulade, a French sauce, is popular all over the world with seafood, French fries, and sandwiches. Its tart, savory, yet smooth character pairs especially well with shellfish.

1 tsp. finely chopped fresh Italian parsley
1 tsp. grated onion
2 hard-boiled large egg yolks
1 tsp. anchovy paste
1 clove garlic, minced

1 large organic egg or equivalent egg substitute
1 cup extra-virgin olive oil
2 tbsp. capers, rinsed, drained, and patted dry
juice of 1/2 lemon, or to your taste

To make the rémoulade, place the parsley, onion, hard-boiled egg yolks, anchovy paste, garlic, and whole egg in a food processor or blender. Process into a paste. With the machine running, slowly add the olive oil in a thin stream through the feed tube until the mixture forms a mayonnaise-like consistency. Fold in the capers and lemon juice. Cover tightly and chill until ready to serve. (You may make the rémoulade up to 24 hours in advance.)

Makes about 1 1/2 cups

aïoli

see variations page 275

An aïoli is a garlicky mayonnaise, first beloved by Provençal cooks and now spread throughout the world. If you are concerned about the use of raw eggs in this sauce, make the Easy Aïoli variation or use egg substitute.

4 large fresh organic egg yolks
4–6 cloves garlic, minced
1/4 tsp. fine kosher or sea salt

1/4 tsp. freshly ground black pepper
1 1/2 cups extra-virgin olive oil

In a food processor, combine the egg yolks, garlic, salt, and pepper. While the motor is running, slowly add the olive oil in a thin stream, creating a mayonnaise-like consistency. Keeps refrigerated for 3–4 days.

Makes about 1 3/4 cups

blender hollandaise

see variations page 276

Serve this wonderful all-purpose sauce on hot grilled, baked, smoked, roasted—you name it—seafood. This recipe is made in the blender or food processor for a quick and easy version of the classic French sauce.

6 large fresh organic egg yolks
2 tbsp. fresh lemon juice
1 tsp. dry mustard
2 sticks (8 oz.) sweet butter, melted and
   still hot

1/4 tsp. cayenne pepper, or to taste
fine kosher or sea salt to taste

Place the egg yolks, lemon juice, and mustard in a food processor or blender, and process until smooth. Drizzle in the hot melted butter, pulsing the food processor or with the blender on low speed, until the sauce thickens. Add the cayenne and season with salt. Keep warm in the top of a double boiler or transfer to a stainless steel bowl and set over a pan of hot, not boiling, water until ready to serve.

Makes about 1 1/2 cups

mango & lime salsa

see variations page 277

Tropical mangoes and fresh lime combine to make a fresh salsa that is delicious with grilled fish and shellfish.

2 cloves garlic, minced
1/4 cup finely chopped onion
1 fresh jalapeño pepper, stemmed, seeded, and
    finely chopped

1/4 cup packed chopped fresh cilantro
2 cups chopped peeled mango
juice of 1 lime, or more to taste
salt and pepper to taste

Combine all ingredients in a bowl. Season to taste and let sit at room temperature until ready to serve. The salsa will keep, covered, in the refrigerator for up to 3 days. Let it come to room temperature before serving.

Makes about 2 cups

baja slaw

see variations page 278

Fresh-tasting and colorful, this slaw goes well with steamed, fried, or grilled seafood.

2 cups shredded red cabbage
2 cups shredded napa cabbage
6 green onions, finely chopped with some of
    the green
1/4 cup tarragon vinegar

1/4 cup sour cream
juice of 1 lime
juice of 1 lemon
kosher salt and freshly ground black pepper
    to taste

In a large bowl, combine the cabbages and green onions. In a small bowl, combine the vinegar, sour cream, and lime and lemon juices. Season to taste. Pour the vinegar mixture over the cabbage and onion mixture and toss to blend. Serve immediately.

Serves 6–8

tomato-spinach orzo

see variations page 279

This colorful pasta dish, made with tiny orzo, can be served hot or cold.

1 lb. orzo, cooked according to package
    directions and drained
1 lb. baby spinach or larger-leafed spinach, torn
    into small pieces
1 pint cherry or grape tomatoes, sliced in half
4 oz. feta cheese, crumbled

4 tbsp. olive oil
1 tbsp. fresh lemon juice
2 cloves garlic, minced
fine kosher or sea salt and freshly ground
    black pepper, to taste

In a large bowl, combine the hot cooked orzo with the spinach, tomatoes, and feta. In a small bowl, whisk the olive oil, lemon juice, and garlic together. Season dressing to taste with the salt and pepper, then pour over the orzo and vegetables, and toss to blend. Serve right away, at room temperature, or chilled.

Serves 4

frites

see variations page 280

Something hot and crispy—like frites or French fries—goes with fish and shellfish like, well, fish and chips! The secret to great frites is to cook them in two stages—once to eliminate moisture, and the second time to get them crispy and golden brown.

8 cups canola oil
2 lbs. medium baking potatoes, peeled
fine kosher or sea salt

Heat 2 inches of oil in a deep fryer or deep saucepan to 325°F. While the oil is heating, cut the potatoes into 1/4-inch sticks. Fry the potatoes in batches for 1 1/2 minutes for each batch. They will be partially cooked, but not golden. Transfer with a slotted spoon to paper towels to drain.

When all the potatoes have been cooked once, increase the temperature to 350°F. Again, fry the potatoes in batches for about 5 minutes each time or until they are crispy and golden brown. Transfer with a slotted spoon to paper towels to drain and season to taste.

Serves 6

coconut rice

see variations page 281

With its taste of the tropics, this rice dish is wonderful with grilled, steamed, fried, baked, or roasted seafood. You can find the coconut and the curry leaves at Asian markets or health food stores.

2 cups water
1 tsp. fine kosher or sea salt
1 cup long-grain rice
1/2 tsp. mustard seeds (optional)
1/8 tsp. dried red pepper flakes

2 bay leaves or 4 curry leaves
1/4 cup vegetable oil
1/2 cup desiccated (not sweetened or flaked) coconut
1/4 cup finely chopped cashews

In a medium saucepan, bring the water and salt to a boil over medium-high heat. Stir in the rice, lower the heat, cover, and simmer for 15 minutes or until tender and the water has been absorbed. While the rice is cooking, combine the mustard seeds, red pepper flakes, bay or curry leaves, and vegetable oil in a large skillet over medium-high heat.

Cook, stirring, until the mustard seeds begin to pop (1–2 minutes). Stir in the coconut and cashews and cook, stirring, until the coconut turns golden and the cashews turn light reddish brown. Stir the mixture into the cooked rice, taste for seasoning, remove the bay or curry leaves, and serve.

Serves 4

variations

ancho-lime butter

see base recipe page 257

cilantro butter
Prepare the basic recipe, using 1/2 cup chopped fresh cilantro and omitting the ground ancho.

fresh herb butter
Prepare the basic recipe, using 1/2 cup chopped mixed fresh herbs such as basil, Italian parsley, marjoram, and dill in place of cilantro. Omit the ground ancho and lime juice. Season to taste with salt.

bistro butter
Prepare the basic recipe, using 1/4 cup chopped mixed fresh herbs such as basil, Italian parsley, marjoram, and dill in place of cilantro. Omit the ground ancho and lime juice. Add 1 tablespoon chopped shallots. Season to taste with salt.

sun-dried tomato butter
Prepare the basic recipe, using 1 tablespoon finely chopped sun-dried tomato packed in oil in place of ground ancho.

variations

herbed tomato vinaigrette

see base recipe page 258

chimichurri sauce
Prepare the basic recipe, omitting the tomatoes and decreasing the salt and pepper to 1/2 teaspoon each.

lemon-dill vinaigrette
Prepare the basic recipe, omitting the tomatoes and decreasing the salt and pepper to 1/2 teaspoon each. Use chopped fresh dill in place of the cilantro, mint, and oregano, and fresh lemon juice in place of the sherry vinegar.

tarragon vinaigrette
Prepare the basic recipe, omitting the tomatoes and decreasing the salt and pepper to 1/2 teaspoon each. Use chopped fresh tarragon in place of the cilantro, mint, and oregano, and tarragon vinegar in place of the sherry vinegar.

tarragon-orange vinaigrette
Prepare the basic recipe, omitting the tomatoes and decreasing the salt and pepper to 1/2 teaspoon each. Use chopped fresh tarragon in place of the cilantro, mint, and oregano, and orange juice in place of the sherry vinegar. Add 1–2 teaspoons grated fresh orange zest.

variations

rémoulade

see base recipe page 261

creole rémoulade
Prepare the basic recipe, adding bottled hot sauce or Cajun seasoning to taste.

shrimp rémoulade
Prepare the basic recipe. Combine 3 cups cooked shrimp with the rémoulade and serve over baby greens.

crab cakes rémoulade
Prepare the basic recipe. Serve drizzled over Crab Cakes (page 105).

rosy rémoulade
Prepare the basic recipe, add 1 tablespoon tomato paste, and stir to blend.

aïoli

see base recipe page 262

easy aïoli
Instead of the basic recipe, put 1 cup mayonnaise in a bowl. Stir in 2
large garlic cloves, minced; 1 teaspoon fresh lemon juice; and salt and
pepper to taste.

easy rouille
Prepare the basic recipe, adding 1/4 teaspoon saffron threads to the
ingredients in the food processor, then process.

classic tartar sauce
Instead of the basic recipe, put 1 cup mayonnaise in a bowl. Stir in 1/4 cup
dill pickle relish and season to taste.

sesame mayonnaise
Instead of the basic recipe, put 1 cup mayonnaise in a bowl. Stir in
1 1/2 teaspoons soy sauce and 1 1/2 teaspoons toasted sesame oil.

variations

blender hollandaise

see base recipe page 264

browned butter hollandaise
Prepare the basic recipe, using butter that has been melted and then cooked until it starts to turn brown.

orange hollandaise
Prepare the basic recipe, adding 1 teaspoon freshly grated orange zest to the ingredients in the blender or food processor.

tarragon hollandaise
Prepare the basic recipe, adding 1 teaspoon dried tarragon and 1 teaspoon tarragon vinegar to the ingredients in the blender or food processor.

ancho-lime hollandaise
Prepare the basic recipe, adding 1 teaspoon freshly grated lime zest and 1 teaspoon ground ancho to the ingredients in the blender or food processor.

mango & lime salsa

see base recipe page 265

pineapple & lime salsa
Prepare the basic recipe, using chopped fresh pineapple in place of mango.

papaya & lime salsa
Prepare the basic recipe, using chopped fresh papaya in place of mango.

watermelon, jicama & lime salsa
Prepare the basic recipe, using 1 cup seeded and chopped watermelon and 1 cup grated jicama in place of mango.

honeydew & lime salsa
Prepare the basic recipe, using chopped honeydew melon in place of mango. Add more fresh lime juice to taste.

variations

baja slaw

see base recipe page 266

zucchini & fennel slaw
Prepare the basic recipe, using grated fresh zucchini in place of red cabbage, thinly sliced fresh bulb fennel in place of green cabbage, and 1/2 cup mayonnaise in place of sour cream.

mustard slaw
Prepare the basic recipe, using 1/2 cup mayonnaise in place of sour cream and 1 tablespoon Dijon mustard in place of lime and lemon juice.

sweet celery seed slaw
Prepare the basic recipe, using 1/2 cup vegetable oil in place of sour cream and 1 tablespoon celery seeds in place of lime and lemon juice. Add 2 tablespoons sugar to the dressing.

lemon-dill slaw
Prepare the basic recipe, using white wine vinegar in place of tarragon and lemon juice in place of lime juice. Add 1 teaspoon dried dill.

variations

tomato–spinach orzo

see base recipe page 268

tomato–arugula orzo
Prepare the basic recipe, using 2 cups baby arugula in place of spinach.

tomato–basil orzo
Prepare the basic recipe, using 1 cup fresh basil leaves in place of spinach
and finely chopped fontina cheese in place of feta.

cucumber–dill orzo
Prepare the basic recipe, using 2 cups chopped cucumber in place of spinach
and 1 cup pitted, chopped Kalamata olives in place of tomatoes. Add 2
teaspoons dried dill weed to the dressing.

butternut squash, sage & parmesan orzo
Prepare the basic recipe, omitting the tomatoes and spinach, and using 2
cups cubed and cooked butternut squash. Use 1 cup freshly grated Parmesan
in place of feta. Sauté 8 fresh sage leaves in olive oil until crisp, and stir into
the Orzo just before serving.

variations

frites

see base recipe page 269

sweet potato fries
Prepare the basic recipe, using sweet potatoes in place of baking potatoes.

parsnip, carrot & potato fries
Prepare the basic recipe, using a mixture of parsnips, large carrots, and baking potatoes in place of potatoes.

saratoga chips
Prepare the basic recipe, slicing the potatoes into 1/4-inch thin rounds instead of sticks.

potato, sweet potato & beet chips
Prepare the basic recipe, using a mixture of baking potatoes, sweet potatoes, and large unpeeled beets in place of potatoes. Slice the vegetables into 1/4-inch thin rounds instead of sticks.

variations

coconut rice

see base recipe page 270

lemon rice
Prepare the basic recipe, adding 1/2 cup chopped green onion, 1/2 cup chopped fresh cilantro, and 1/4 cup chopped green chile in place of the coconut. Fry until the vegetables are softened and cashews are reddish brown. Stir the mixture into the rice along with 1/4 cup fresh lemon juice.

saffron rice
Prepare the basic recipe, adding 1/2 teaspoon saffron threads to the rice as it is cooking. Omit the coconut.

tex-mex rice
Cook the rice according to the basic recipe. Instead of all the other ingredients, stir in 1 cup chopped canned tomato with green chiles, undrained, 1/4 cup chopped fresh cilantro, 1/2 cup crumbed queso fresco, and 1 tablespoon Ancho-Lime Butter (page 257). Season to taste.

cilantro rice
Cook the rice according to the basic recipe. Instead of all the other ingredients, stir in 1 cup chopped fresh cilantro and 2 tablespoons fresh lime juice. Season to taste.

index

A

aïoli 262–3, 275
  platters 70
alder-planked tilapia with
  artichoke glaze
  184–5, 197
almond-crusted salmon
  roasted corn relish
  223
amberjack
  Asian-style 170
  roast in sherry
    marinade 227
  sashimi 28–9
ancho-lime butter 257,
  272
ancho–lime hollandaise
  276
angels on horseback 143
apple-smoked salmon
  238, 250
archangels on horseback
  143
artichoke, shrimp & red
  bell pepper pizza 145
Asian-style
  amberjack 170
  fish soup, easy 94
  raw fish salad 26–7,
    40
  roast trout 228
asparagus & shrimp
  sushi 43

Aussie-style
  calamari 116
  seafood soup 94

B

bacon-wrapped roast
  trout 228
baja fish tacos 162–3,
  174
baja seafood & vegetable
  wraps 67
baja slaw 266–7, 278
baked fish 140–1, 151
  in banana leaves 68
  halibut en papillote
    135, 147
  scallops en coquille
    127, 143
baking 19
Balinese shrimp satay 169
banana leaf-wrapped
  barramundi 138, 149
Barbados-style
  fried fish 113, 124
  leaf-wrapped fish 149
  pompano 170
barramundi
  banana leaf-wrapped
    138, 149
  macadamia-buttered
    182–3, 196
Basque-style roast fish
  217, 228

bay scallops
  crudo 42
  en coquille 143
bayou-smoked catfish 'n'
  corn 244–5, 255
  soup 255
beachside grilled
  mackerel 156–7, 170
Béarnaise-style fried
  fish 124
beer-battered fish 'n'
  chips 108, 120
Belgian mussel stew 96
bistro butter 272
blender hollandaise 264,
  276
bluefish
  beachside grilled 170
  roast with coriander
    & bay 216, 227
boiling 48
bouillabaisse 75
brandade de morue
  136–7, 148
branzino
  Korean roasted
    218–19, 229
  roasted with tapas
    topping 229
browned butter
  hollandaise 276
butter-poached lobster
  60

butternut squash, sage &
  parmesan orzo 279
butters 272

C

Cajun calamari 116
calamari, flash-fried
  101, 116
California roll sushi 43
campfire trout 158–9, 171
Cap d'Antibes-style fish
  soup 90
Cartagena-style
  fried lobster 124
  paella 72
catfish
  cornmeal-fried 109,
    121
  in banana leaves 68
  pecan-crusted with
    roasted corn relish
    210–11, 223
  smoked
    bayou 'n' corn
      244–5, 255
    hot dip 255
    low-country & rice
      255
  stir-grilled 176
cedar-planked sole
  roulade 191, 202
ceviche 34, 45
chaudreé 91

chili-basted Indonesian shrimp 169
chimichurri sauce 273
Chinese-style
  fish in banana leaves 68
  seafood dumplings 57, 69
  seafood soup 82, 94
cilantro butter 272
cilantro rice 281
cilantro-saffron zarzuela 98
clams
  bake 73
  chowder 76–7, 91
  & corn chowder 91
  sake-steamed 66
  steamed with casino butter 66
  strips, flash-fried 116
cockle curry laksa 99
coconut
  green curry shrimp flatbread 145
  laksa 99
  prawn salad 119
  prawns & jezebel sauce 106–7, 119
  rice 270–1, 281
cod
  dried salt, brandade de morue 136–7, 148
  maple-planked 192–3, 203
  smoked, with hollandaise 253

steamed in banana leaves 56
cold smoking 20
coquilles St. Jacques 143
  purses 144
cornmeal-fried catfish 109, 121
crab
  & artichoke casserole 150
  cakes 104–5, 118
    rémoulade 274
  California roll sushi 43
  cocktail 64
  dip, classic 127, 142
  dumplings 69
  quiche 146
  Rangoon 69
  salad, easy 65
  & shrimp bisque 92
  steamed 50–1, 65
crab-stuffed mushrooms 142
crawfish, boiled 64
creole style
  rémoulade 274
  roasted shrimp & pepper po' boy 220
  snapper 97
crustless seafood quiche 146
cucumber sushi 43
cucumber-dill orzo 279
curried shrimp dip 142
cuttlefish roasted in sherry marinade 222

D
deep-fryers 12
dill & beet-cured gravlax 44

E
equipment 12–15

F
finger sushi 43
fish 'n' chips 108, 120
fish cakes 118
fish curry, Kerala 83, 95
fish fillets, butter-poached 71
fish gratin 151
fish molee 95
fish soup
  Chinese 94
  Thai lemongrass 93
  see also soups
fish steaks, butter-poached 71
fish tacos 162–3, 174
flash-fried calamari 101, 116
flying fish, Barbados-style fried 113, 124
French fries 269, 280
French style
  fish gratin 151
  roast turbot 225
  scallop gratin 151
freshness 6, 8–9
fried fish 100–25

Barbados-style 113, 124
  clam roll 116
frites 269, 280
fritto misto with salsa verde 110–11
frogmore stew 73
frying 17

G
gravlax 32–3, 44
grill racks 18
grilled fish 17–8, 152–77
  halibut with papaya salsa 161, 173
  mini tuna "burgers" with rémoulade 152–3, 168
  oysters with salsa verde 38
  snapper aotearoa 46
  swordfish with tomato-spinach orzo 66–7, 177
  yabbies with ginger-lime sauce 160, 172
grilling planks 15, 19
grouper, Barbadian leaf-wrapped 149

H
haddock
  kedgeree 243, 254
  maple-planked with onion butter 203
  with hollandaise 242, 253

hake
    harissa-planked with fresh salsa 197
    roasted with artichoke glaze 223
    tapas-style 124
halibut
    crudo 30, 42
    en papillote 135, 147
    grilled with papaya salsa 161, 173
    on the grill 147
    poached 70
    roasted red bell pepper relish 223
    roasted romesco 224
    simple sushi 31
    steamed in banana leaves 56
hardwood chips 12
hardwood planks 15, 19
harissa-planked hake with fresh salsa 197
herb butter 272
herbed tomato vinaigrette 258–9, 273
hollandaise, blender 264, 276
honeydew & lime salsa 277
hot smoked catfish dip 255
hot smoking 20

I
Indonesian style
    shrimp & chile soup 93
    shrimp & peanut wraps 67
Italian style
    baked fish 151
    roast fish 214–17, 226
    roast shrimp 226

J
Jamaican roast turbot 213, 225
Japanese fish soup 94
John Dory, aotearoa 35

K
katong laksa 99
kedgeree 243, 254
    cakes 254
    stuffed tomatoes 254
Kerala fish curry 83, 95
kingfish roast with coriander & bay 227
Korean roasted branzino 218–19, 229

L
lake perch, cornmeal-fried 121
leaf-wrapped
    fish 149
    smoked shrimp with rémoulade 231, 246
    trout, grilled 171

Lebanese baked fish 151
lemon rice 281
lemon-dill slaw 278
lemon-dill vinaigrette 273
lobster
    baja tacos 174
    bisque 78–9, 92
    butter-poached 60
    cakes 118
    laksa 99
    mac & cheese 150
    poblano & mango ceviche 45
    purses 130–1, 144
    quiche 134, 146
    seashore dinner 62–3
    steamed 65
    Venetian roast 226
low-country smoked catfish & rice 255
low-fat sole 123

M
macadamia-buttered barramundi 182–3, 196
mackerel
    grilled 156–7, 170
    roast with coriander & bay 227
    simple sushi 31
mahi mahi
    ceviche 34
    planked 188–9, 200
    stir-grilled 176

Malaysian leaf-wrapped snapper 149
mango & lime salsa 265, 277
Manhattan-style clam chowder 91
maple-planked cod & new potatoes with onion butter 192–3, 203
maple-smoked whitefish soup 252
    with butternut squash orzo 240–1, 252
    marinading 18
Mexican roast trout 228
monkfish
    planked 186, 198
    roasted romesco 212, 224
    seared 175
    soup with rouille 224
Moroccan baked fish 140–1, 151
mussels
    chowder 91, 249
    pasta with basil aïoli 249
    Singaporean laksa 88–9, 99
    steamed in white wine 52–3, 66
    with frites & aïoli 236–7, 249
mustard slaw 278

N

New Orleans-style fish
soup 90
Niçoise fish on a plank
187, 199
nigiri sushi 43

O

octopus, roasted in sherry
marinade 208–9, 222
oil heat test 17
orange grove snapper 46
orange hollandaise 276
orange roughy
maple-planked 203
roasted with lemon-
tarragon butter 229
orange-zested gravlax 44
orzos 268, 279
oven planks 15, 19
overcooking, to avoid 16
oysters
coconut with jezebel
sauce 119
grilled, with salsa
verde 38
& leek chowder 221
leek penne 221
on the half shell 23,
38
pan roast with
buttery leeks 206–7,
221
po' boy sandwich 117
& sausage stew 96

smoked
po' boy sandwich
232–3, 247
stew 247
stovetop-smoked
247
stew 84–5, 96

P

paella, easy 61, 71
pancetta-wrapped perch
171
papaya & lime salsa 277
Parisian-style fish soup 90
parsnip, carrot & potato
fries 280
pecan-crusted catfish
with roasted corn
relish 210–11, 223
perch
lake perch, cornmeal-
fried 121
pancetta-wrapped
171
pesto-planked 197
plated 68
Peruvian ceviche 34, 45
Peruvian shrimp &
almond paella 72
pesce al forno 214–17,
226
pesto-planked perch 197
pineapple & lime salsa
277
planked fish 19
mahi mahi with

pineapple salsa
188–9, 200
monkfish tapas 186,
198
salmon chimichurri
180–1, 195
shrimp with bistro
butter 179, 194
tilapia with artichoke
glaze 184–5, 197
plated perch 68
po' boy sandwiches 117,
247
creole roasted shrimp
& pepper 220
smoked oyster po' boy
sandwich 232–3,
247
poaching 20, 48
halibut 70
salmon 58–9, 70
pomfret, steamed in
banana leaves 56
pompano, Barbadian 170
potato, sweet potato &
beet chips 280
preparation tips 16–20
prosciutto-wrapped
scallops 175
Provençal fish soup with
rouille 75, 90
Puerto Rican paella 72

Q

quiches 134, 146

R

rainforest leaf-wrapped
fish 149
in banana leaves 68
raw fish
Asian salad 26–7, 40
slicing 20
red snapper
aotearoa 35
on a bed of mango 97
stir-fried with orange
oil 114–17, 125
veracruzano 86, 97
rémoulade 260–1, 274
rice 270–1, 281
roast fish 19
baby octopus in
sherry marinade
208–9, 222
bluefish with
coriander & bay
216, 227
jerk salmon 225
monkfish romesco
212, 224
shrimp & asparagus
205, 220
tapas-style 228
rosy rémoulade 274
rouille, easy 275
rum & lime-grilled shrimp
on the barbie 154–5,
169

S

saffron rice 281
sake-steamed clams 66
salmon
    Asian raw fish salad
        40
    "burgers" 168
    carpaccio 39
    crudo with carpaccio
        sauce 42
    curry, Kerala 95
    dumplings, Chinese 69
    en papillote 147
    gravlax 32–3, 44
    planked 180–1, 195
    poached 58–9, 70
    roasted jerk 225
    sashimi 28–9, 41
    simple sushi 31
    smoked
        aïoli salad 250
        apple-smoked 238,
            250
        cakes 250
        scrambled eggs 250
        smoke-planked
            lemon 201
        & snow peas, stir-
            fried 125
        stir-grilled 165, 176
    tartare 47
salsas 265, 277
Samoan snapper 46
saratoga chips 280
sardines roast with
    coriander & bay 227

sashimi 28–9, 41
    seared 41
satay sauce 169
sautéd sole with browned
    butter hollandaise
    112, 123
scallops
    & asparagus, roasted
        220
    coquilles St. Jacques
    purses 144
        en coquille 127, 143
        gratin 151
        planked with bistro
            butter 194
    planked with
        honeydew salsa 200
    prosciutto-wrapped
        175
    roasted in sherry
        marinade 222
    rum & lime-grilled on
        the barbie 169
    seared 164, 175
    smoked
        chowder 248
        pasta with bistro
            butter 248
        po' boy sandwich
            247
        with tomato-
            spinach orzo 234–5,
            248
    smoke-planked
        lemon-tarragon 201

stovetop-smoked
    248
soup, Thai lemongrass
    93
stir-fried with
    fragrant orange oil
    125
scrambled eggs
    smoked salmon 250
    smoked trout 251
sea bass on the grill 147
sea scallops on the half
shell 38
seafood
    dumplings 57, 69
    easy paella 61, 71
    fritto misto 122
    soup, Chinese 82, 94
    & vegetable wraps,
        Thai 54–5
    wontons 69
    zarzuela 87, 98
seared fish
    gravlax 44
    monkfish 175
    sashimi 41
    scallops 164, 175
seashore lobster dinner
    62–3
sesame mayonnaise 275
shellfish
    fritto misto 122
    stock 65
shrimp
    & artichoke casserole
        139, 150

    pot pies 150
    & asparagus
        roasted 205, 220
        sushi 43
    baja tacos 174
    beer-battered 120
    beignets 117
    bruschetta 220
    butter-poached 71
    chili-basted
    Indonesian 169
    chipotle ceviche 45
    cocktail 49, 64
    coconut, & jezebel
        sauce 106–7, 119
    coconut prawn salad
        119
    curry, Kerala 95
    dip 142
    flatbread, Thai 132–3,
        145
    grilled with ginger-
        lime sauce 160, 172
    Italian roast 226
    mac & cheese 150
    pan-roasted with
        buttery leeks 221
    & peanut wraps,
        Indonesian 67
    planked 179, 194
        with mango salsa
            200
    rémoulade 274
    roasted
        in sherry marinade
            222

romesco 224
rum & lime-grilled on the barbie 154–5, 169
smoked 64
  leaf-wrapped 231, 246
  po' boy sandwich 247
  stovetop-smoked 246
  smoke-planked lemon 201
  soup, Thai lemongrass 80–1, 93
  stir-fried with fragrant orange oil 125
  stir-grilled 176
  teppanyaki 169
  veracruzano 97
  vindaloo 95
simmering 20
Singapore-style steamed fish in banana leaves 56, 68
Singaporean laksa 88–9, 99
skillet-grilled trout 171
skin side, identifying 16
slaws 266–7, 278
slicing raw fish 20
smelts, fritto misto 110–11
smoke-planked lemon-tarragon snapper 190, 201

smoked fish 20
catfish dip 255
cod with hollandaise 253
haddock
  kedgeree 243, 254
  with hollandaise 242, 253
mussels
  chowder 249
  with frites & aïoli 236–7, 249
  pasta with basil aïoli 249
oysters
  po' boy sandwich 232–3, 247
  stew 247
salmon
  aïoli salad 250
  Asian raw fish salad 40
  cakes 118, 250
  scrambled eggs 250
scallops
  chowder 248
  pasta with bistro butter 248
  po' boy sandwich 247
  with tomato-spinach orzo 234–5, 248
shrimps
  cocktail 64

leaf-wrapped 231, 246
po' boy sandwich 247
snapper, smoke-planked lemon tarragon 190, 201
trout pâté 251
  salad 251
  scrambled eggs 251
  with fresh herb butter 239, 251
whitefish beignets 252
see also stovetop-smoked fish
snapper 46
  aotearoa 35, 46
  creole 97
  Malaysian leaf-wrapped 149
  planked lemon-tarragon 190, 201
sole
  fritto misto 110–11
  orange-buttered on a plank 196
  roulades 191, 202
  sautéd 112
Sonoran paella 72
soul succotash 73
soups & stews 74–99
southern fried tilapia 121
southern-style shrimp & bacon quiche 146
Spanish roast turbot in

sherry marinade 225
spot shrimp, grilled 172
squid
  chaudreé 91
  flash-fried 101
  fritto misto 110–11
  roasted in sherry marinade 222
  sashimi 41
steamed fish 20, 48
  clams with casino butter 66
  crab 50–1, 65
  in banana leaves 56, 68
  lobster 65
  stir-fried red snapper with orange oil 114–17, 125
stir-grilled fish
  pacific rim mahi mahi 176
  salmon with cherry tomatoes & sugar snap peas 165, 176
  shrimp satay 176
stovetop smoked fish 15
  oysters 247
  scallops 248
  shrimp 246
substitution chart 10–11
sun-dried tomato butter 272
sushi
  mats 15
  simple 31, 43

sweet celery seed slaw
278
sweet potato fries 280
swordfish
baja tacos 174
burgers with tarragon
hollandaise 168
ceviche 34
crudo with tapenade
42
grilled 166–7, 177

T
tapas 153
planked monkfish
186, 198
tapas-style hake 124
tapas-style roast fish
228
topping 186
tarragon
hollandaise 276
vinaigrette 273
tartar sauce 275
tartare tower 47
tartare trio 47
tex-mex rice 281
Thai-style
fried fish 124
grilled halibut 173
lemongrass shrimp
soup 80–1, 93
seafood & vegetable
wraps 54–5, 67
shrimp flatbread
132–3, 145
snapper 46

thermometers 15
tilapia
alder-planked 184–5,
197
ceviche 45
roasted pecan-crusted
with basil aïoli 223
southern fried 121
steamed in banana
leaves 56
tartare trio 47

tomato–arugula orzo 279
tomato–basil orzo 279
tomato–spinach orzo
268, 279
trout
campfire 158–9, 171
cilantro-buttered on a
plank 196
en papillote 147
grilled bacon-
wrapped 171
roast 217, 228
sashimi 28–9, 41
smoked 251
with fresh herb
butter 239, 251
tuna
Asian raw fish salad
26–7, 40
baja tacos 174
"burgers" 152–3, 168
carpaccio 24–5, 39
ceviche 34, 45
Niçoise on a plank
187, 199

sashimi 28–9, 41
simple sushi 31
tartare trio 47
turbot
pistachio-buttered on
a plank 196
roast 213, 225

V
Venetian roast lobster
226

vichyssoise–style oyster
stew 96
vinaigrettes 273

W
walleye
maple-smoked 252
pecan-buttered on a
plank 196
watermelon, jicama &
lime salsa 277
white clam pizza 145
whitebait, fritto misto
110–11
whitefish
beignets 102–3, 117
maple-planked with
three-pepper butter
203
roasted with three-
pepper butter 229
smoked
beignets 252
soup 252

with butternut
squash orzo 240–1,
252
wine-battered fish with
hollandaise 120
wok grills 12
woo hoo grilled halibut
with papaya salsa
161,173
wood chips 12

Y
yellowtail
Asian raw fish salad
26–7
kingfish aotearoa 35
tartare in tortilla
cones 36–7, 47
yu sheng 26–7, 40

Z
zarzuelas 87, 98
zucchini & fennel slaw
278